City Cycling

Richard Ballantine

snowbooks
LONDON

Proudly published in the UK, in 2007, by:
Snowbooks Ltd.
120 Pentonville Road
London
N1 9JN
Tel: 0207 837 6482
Fax: 0207 837 6348
email: info@snowbooks.com
www.snowbooks.com
SMALL PUBLISHER OF THE YEAR 2006

British Library Cataloguing in Publication Data
A catalogue record for this book is available from the British Library.

ISBN 13 978-1-905005-604

www.citycycling.org

I. CITY CYCLING

II. WHEEL DEALING

III. TACTICS

IV. RIDING

V. MECHANICS

Dedication

For the love of my life — Sherry!

Richard Ballantine is a cycling author and advocate. His *Richard's Bicycle Book* appeared in 1972, at the time of a boom in bike sales stimulated by a world wide oil crisis, and became an essential handbook for millions of cyclists. Richard's classic 'manual of bicycle maintenance and enjoyment' was (and still is) enthusiastic, friendly, and colourful, and utterly uncompromising in championing cyclists as first-class road users, equally important as motorists. This is now the conventional view.

Richard rode on to found several cycling magazines, and author numerous books on cycling, many translated all over the world. A mountain bike pioneer in the UK, and a participant in the human power vehicle movement since the 1980s, Richard is chair of the British Human Power Club and of the International Human Powered Vehicle Association, and a founder member of the Human Power Institute, publisher of the Human Power eJournal.

Born in the USA, Richard is resident in England with his wife Sherry, and the latest family member: Sunshine 'Sunny' Ballantine, a fast-growing F2 Labradoodle.

ACKNOWLEDGEMENTS

Mike Burrows (left): 'Richard, you're rubbish on a race track, but you can drop racers in traffic — why don't you do a book on city cycling?'
Richard (right): 'Good idea!'

* * *

Richard: 'Guys, my cycling book needs pictures . . .?'
Shawn Ballantine and Lenin Arvelo (photographers), Kathy Ballantine, Danielle Ballantine and Henrike Reinsberger (models): 'We'll help!'
And they did!

Henny

Danny

Kathy – and Sunny!

Kathy and Henny

Shawn

Lenin

Thanks to Stuart Dennison of Bikefix, and Grant Young of Condor Cycles, for supplying photographs, help with bikes and bits, and good cheer. These valuable people do constant good work for cycling, at every level from helping beginning riders to supporting major races and events.

Stuart

Grant

Special thanks to Emma Barnes, MD and publisher of Snowbooks. Em's drive, warm spirit, and complete involvement in every phase of book-making are extraordinary. Em took many of the pictures for *City Cycling* and did the design of the book, all while still doing the 1001 things involved in running an exciting, award-winning publishing house.

I: CITY CYCLING

This book is about cycling for transport in cities. If you are interested in racing, mountain biking, or touring far lands, try the reading list at the back of this book. If you want to learn about city cycling and making the most of urban living, you are on the right wheel. Stay close!

As transport, cycling has a unique advantage: you can speed up or slow down, stop, or change a journey, as and when you please. This flexibility perfectly complements the varied geographic and demographic nature of cities. On a bike you can speed miles across town, but change pace to cruise a street of interesting-looking restaurants, follow a tantalising aroma of baking doughnuts to source, or pause for a chat with a friend.

Yet cycling also purely shines for speed. Transport is about movement, and in cities, for distances up to 6 miles, bikes are faster than anything else going. Most urban journeys are short: in London, half are under a mile, and 85 percent are under 5 miles — by bike, half an hour at a sedate 10 MPH, and just 20 minutes at a crisp 15 MPH. Ever done a 5-mile journey by tube in 20 minutes? By bus?!

Bikes are fine for longer journeys, as well. Once you have your legs, distances of 7 to 10 miles and even more are enjoyable. A brilliant technique is mixed-mode transport. You cycle, say, to a train station, ride the rails, and then cycle again to your destination. And if (as happens often) something goes wrong with the train, you can beam a big grin, because while others queue for buses or pound shoe leather, you are off and away on your bike.

Reliability is an intrinsic and important advantage of cycling. Part of the fun of living in cities is diversity and doing lots of different things. For this to work one needs to be places on time; lateness is self-defeating. Cities are crowded and often congested, so if you rely on public transport or a car to get around, then you must allow extra time for delays. Go by bike, and time is yours. Late? Just step on it! You cannot make a bus or train go faster, but you surely can hustle a bike.

The money is good, too. Living in Britain costs a bomb. Never mind the many millions of people enslaved in menial jobs at minimum wage levels or less. People making pretty good money — teachers, firemen, nurses, and other professionals — have a hard time making ends meet. Food and shelter costs are sky-high, and every form of transport bar cycling or walking is more expensive than anywhere in the world except Japan. In an average British household, 18 to 20 percent of income is spent on transport. That is not just incredible. It is damaging to the national economy in general and your existence in particular. People who equate cycling with impoverishment have their heads screwed front to back. It is the other way round. Ride a bike, and, financially, you enjoy an instant upgrade!

Cars? Please, no. Not in cities. Cars and lorries are fine when journey distances are long or difficult and there is no other way, and for hauling bricks and pianos. But as private transport in cities, cars are slow, expensive, and thoroughly aggravating. Do the TV ads show cars stuck motionless in traffic? Motorists being fleeced with fines? Don't be hoodwinked. Cars are no fun in cities. People who live in high density metropolitan areas increasingly do not own cars. They use car-share pools, or rent motor vehicles as required.

Cycling means pedalling. Yes! This is good for you. Cyclists drink at the Fountain of Youth; they live for years longer, and more importantly, they live healthier and enjoy life more. There is no greater gift.

Last on a short list of advantages, and naturally not least: cycling sharpens your being. You do for yourself. You take charge. As a result, you are more aware and switched-on, and this tends to carry over into the rest of your existence — work, play, social consciousness, and even your love life!

♂SEX♀SEX♂SEX♀SEX♂SEX♀SEX♂SEX♀SEX♂SEX♀

The sex drive is our most primary instinct, and the effect of cycling on sexuality has been a topic of endless fascination ever since the invention of the bicycle. Victorians fantasised (hopefully) that cycling would erotically stimulate females, and the first women to wear trousers for cycling were regarded as exceedingly daring and risqué. More recent medical studies have gone the other way, reporting that cycling can inhibit or reduce sexual drive and performance.

What is the story? Cycling promotes fitness and better health, which may facilitate more active and/or better sex. However, cyclists of both genders riding upright bikes do need to take care of their genitals. Women are (I am told) sensitive in this area, and can be hurt by impacts from bumps, or numbed by continual pressure on the genitals. One remedy is a soft, padded saddle, but a better solution is a saddle with a hole or slot in the middle to relieve pressure on the genitals. There are many models on the market; any women experiencing discomfort with a standard saddle should immediately try a more design-specific model.

Men are (I know for a fact) sensitive in the genital area. A whack to the goolies, while acutely painful, is unlikely to cause more than a short-term reduction in sexual performance. However, long hours in the saddle can pinch and deaden the nerves in the crotch, which can result in numbness in the genital region and/or failure to obtain or maintain an erection. The solution is the same as for women; reduce pressure. First trick: stand up out of the saddle often. Second trick: lower the nose of the saddle a little. You don't want to go too far with this and be pitched forward off your perch, but a change of as little as a degree or two may make a vital difference. If adjusting the tilt of the saddle does not do it, then change to a saddle with a groove or recess down the centre. With the pressure off, rides will be better, on and off the bike.

The bicycle was an instrumental tool for female emancipation. These Victorian ladies are having a fine time sending up a range of taboos — smoking, working on machines, and showing a bit of leg.

Critical Mass

Cycling is great, but what about the risk of being mangled or killed by a car? This is what stops most people from cycling. There is a risk of harm, absolutely, but it is diminishing. In fact, using a bike is itself a positive move toward safety. Why? Because cycling in Britain is at critical mass.

Critical Mass Ride, San Francisco, 2005

Critical Mass bike rides began in San Francisco, California, and have become popular all over the world. Hundreds, sometimes thousands, of cyclists assemble and ride as a group. For a while, the cyclists own the road. Motorists and the press sometimes perceive the rides as deliberate attempts to screw up traffic. Not so. The Critical Mass slogan is: 'We are traffic'. That is the status cyclists must have in order to be safe.

In the Netherlands the cycle/car crash rate is just 10 percent of the rate in Britain. Is this because the Dutch have a lovely system of cycle paths? No, the cycle paths are only a swell bonus. Forty percent of work commuting journeys are by bike. It is not just the cycle paths that teem with cyclists. Dutch roads and streets have cyclists like Trafalgar Square has pigeons. Motorists are considerate of cyclists, because they have to be. There is no other possibility.

Critical Mass meet at London's South Bank on the last Friday of each month

The story in other countries with large numbers of cyclists, such as Denmark and Germany, is the same. High levels of cycle usage mean low cycle/car crash rates. For UK cyclists, the important factor is that the relationship between the cycle usage rate and the cycle/car crash rate is not an even progression. Once the number of work commuting journeys by bike reaches around nine percent, a modest further increase in cycle usage triggers a proportionately far larger decrease in the crash rate. In short, a critical mass of cyclists triggers a dramatic change — exactly where we are now.

Danish cycling policy

This extensive survey, based on a census taken in Copenhagen and on calculations of number of trips cycled along the major roads in 2000, shows that as the number of kilometres cycled increases, the number of serious cyclist injuries decreases.

Source: Cykelpolitik 2002-2012: City of Copenhagen, Building and Administration, Roads and Parks Department 2002

Hop on a bike and join the revolution! It is all happening. Cycling advocates have been promoting cycling for years. Even the government is awake to the idea. Cycling is definitely becoming easier and safer, but still, riding in Britain is nothing like as advanced as in Holland, Denmark, or Germany. As well, conditions vary by towns and local areas. Accordingly, the cycling techniques and strategies that will work for you need to be tailored to circumstances, and to your skill level and temperament.

Cycling hot-spot at rush hour

SCARED?

Scared in traffic? So am I! It is sensible to be scared. The issue is what to do about it. To feel better, you need to learn how to cope with traffic. The process takes time and experience. The crucial principle to understand is that your safety is under your control. You set the pace, and tyro or expert, you mix humility with courage; you are always both a little cautious — and brave.

Attaining the understanding and skills for riding with confidence and genuine happiness is not always easy. Even very good riders sometimes experience problems. Still, for better or worse, this is your life, and you should make the most of it. Whatever the conditions, and whatever your ability and confidence, remember, you were born free, and are free. Especially on a bike. The streets and roads and the world are as much yours as anyone's. Cut your own show. Celebrate your birthright!

Lifestyle!

Cycling enriches the quality of life. I mean life in general, not just the good things cycling does for you in particular. A bike is naturally handy for local errands: calling at the butcher for the cold cuts you like, or the bakery that has fresh bread, or the swell coffee shop where the owner roasts beans every day. Farmer's market? Made for you. On a bike you get used to cherry-picking, to enjoying the pleasure of having exactly what you want. And not incidentally, a whole bunch of other good things happen as well.

Local shopping means more contact with people as individuals. Humans. Remember them? They come in rich variety, and when you see and deal with people in small shops and businesses, the contact is flavoured with genuine courtesy and awareness. Behaving

Camden Coffee Shop

nicely is part of the fabric of existence.

Dealing with individuals and small enterprises helps support a type of economy that is good for a neighbourhood community. Big chain stores may pay wages to local employees, but profits and capital go elsewhere.

Local businesses and shops are run by people who spend their money and energies where they live. This makes a big difference to the quality of life, in just about every way that counts — from active involvement in schools and libraries and other civic activities and institutions, to safety on the streets.

Off To Work We Go . . .

Darwin's Deli is one of several thriving firms using fleets of bike trailers to deliver luncheon sandwiches and treats to shops, businesses, offices, and institutions all over London. Motor vehicles could not achieve the same comprehensive level of door-to-door coverage, nor provide employment for as many people. For economy and efficiency, many home delivery food firms are also now switching from mopeds and scooters to bikes.

Photo: Tom Bogdanowicz

On a wider scale, local-business economies are better for the planet. Big chain stores sell goods cheaply by using massive amounts of energy in manufacturing and distribution. A factory-farm head of lettuce has a large energy cost for fertilisers and farm equipment, and then for preservation and distribution over great distances. By comparison, a locally-grown lettuce may require more manual labour in hoeing and watering, but the net energy cost to land it on your plate is much less. (It will also, as food, have more zip.)

Newspaper clipping from the Evening Standard:

2   ★★★★   Evening Standard Tuesday, 8

This shopping trolley of food took 245,900 miles to get here

(That's further than a trip to the moon)

MILES TRAVELLED BY FOOD IN OUR BASKET

Item	Origin	Mileage
Spinach salad	Spain	800
Grapes	South Africa	6,000
Blackberries	Mexico	5,500
Strawberries	Egypt	2,600
Blueberries	Chile	7,300
Apricots	New Zealand	12,000
Nectarines	Chile	7,300
Figs	Argentina	7,000
Mango	Peru	6,300
Lime	Brazil	5,500
Avocados	Israel	2,400
Apples	USA	4,500
...on the cob	Thailand	6,000

BY ELIZABETH HOPKIRK

SUPERMARKETS and shoppers are today blamed for the vast mileage behind the groceries in an average weekly shop.

It follows calls for supermarkets to label products with the number of "food miles" they have travelled, to enable shoppers to make more informed purchases.

When the Evening Standard bought a trolley of food from one supermarket,

basis is to eat, because our actions affect farms, landscapes and food businesses."

The food and drink bought by the Standard came from 20 different countries. Each item had travelled 7,000 miles on average. Although some of our purchases can only be grown abroad,

Long distance: campaigners say transporting food across continents harms th

Could You Be The N

From the Evening Standard

Why is this important? In simple terms, two reasons: climate change and common humanity. Energy use and pollution are the drivers of climate change and a set of problems far more consequential and life threatening than any prospect of war. As for common humanity, we live in a world where a billion people are outright starving for food and water. In such circumstances, over-consumption is gross. We can cut back a little without hardship. What it means to others is life.

Riding a bike will not solve all the world's problems. But it does start to tickle at the kinds of changes we need in order to survive and prosper. And, hey, you know about little acorns and mighty oaks. It is simple, and it is true: when you cycle, you both enjoy and help create a better world.

How To Use This Book

Directions for assembling and using barbecues and moon rockets always say to read the instructions all the way through and understand the whole picture before you make a move. You are not heading for the moon, but setting up for urban cycling requires sorting a lot of variables. You've got to analyse your situation, the kinds of journeys you will be taking, the conditions you will encounter, the budget, the parking situation, and a whole bunch of other factors, any of which can have a big effect on what sort of bike or bikes and set-up is best for you.

Many people start with a notion of the kind of bike they would like to have: a high-tech, full suspension mountain bike, perhaps, or a glittering, finely-honed lightweight road racer, or even one of those sexy-looking laid-back recumbent cycles. Everyday riding will just be a side benefit. Good dream, but start again!

Make everyday riding the main agenda. A conscious appreciation of the lifestyle you want and tailoring the machine to suit will make the whole business a lot more successful and enjoyable. Simple example: you want to commute to work and discover there is a good route via a canal towpath. You need a bike with wide, supple tyres and possibly suspension as well, to take the sting out of bumps and uneven surfaces. You do not need a bike with thin, hard tyres and a stiff ride. Simple — sure. But important!

So, please, read through the whole book. Scan some bits if you want, but get an overview of all the factors to think about when setting up for urban cycling. There are numerous options, and more than one may be of interest. That's fine: keep in mind that you can have more than one machine ...

Kinds of Journeys

Bikes open up a wider world than most motorists, users of public transport, and even pedestrians, ever see. With a bike you can go fast, meander, or dismount and walk. You can vary routes and riding styles to suit your mood and the day.

There are five principal kinds of routes or riding scenes:

1. Main roads and streets used by most vehicles. Provided that traffic is flowing freely, the primary advantage is speed. Once you have your legs, you can push a bike along at a pretty good clip — 14 to 16 MPH on a decent upright lightweight, 20 MPH or faster on an aerodynamic recumbent. In general, the best going is on main thoroughfares where you can keep up momentum.

Main roads are fast, and usually smoother, too.

In busy traffic you need to behave as a proper road vehicle. That means understanding what is happening, and participating in give and take with other road users in such a way as to be courteous while asserting and holding your rightful place in the scheme of things. Mainline traffic riding is fun exactly because it is dynamic and engaging, and oddly enough, it scores well on safety. Riding within a strong stream of traffic helps protect you. Cross-traffic is better-behaved; motorists who might pull out in front of a lone cyclist will wait their turn if several vehicles are coming along. As well, on busy roads cyclists are less vulnerable to interference from pedestrians and random events.

2. Secondary roads and streets with light motor vehicle traffic. These are beloved of cycle-route planners and often are very good. You go in comparative peace. On the debit side, cross-traffic may be less considerate of cyclists, and some motor vehicles sharing the route may be moving fast. There can be other surprises, too, and in general, secondary routes work best at a more relaxed pace. Believe, as a cyclist this is often exactly what one wants and needs!

Cycle Route, Secondary Street, Primrose Hill, London

It's a busy place, with lots of potential surprises. Ride such streets at an easy pace.

Secondary and back-routes are nice for the parts of a journey that involve climbing at slow speeds. They are sometimes quicker than main routes, because you can often use short-cuts not open to motor vehicles. My neighbourhood has several roads that prohibit direct entry by cars, but not by bikes.

3. Cycle paths and back streets marked for cyclists. These have definite pros and cons. If you prefer to ride slow and easy and dislike cars, cycle paths can be good. If you want to move along, they are confining. Most urban cycle paths are not well designed; they take torturous twists and turns, are too narrow, have inane hazards such as lamp posts bang in the middle of the path, and other shortcomings. As well, some go through neighbourhoods where cyclists are prone to assault.

And yet, cycle paths have their uses. One of them is segregation from motor vehicles, and there are times and places — rush hour on a dark, rainy night when visibility is limited — when this is more comfortable than running with the main traffic. However, many so-called segregated cycle paths are very dangerous, because they cut across mainstream traffic flows in ways that motorists cannot understand or anticipate.

Cycle transportation engineering in Britain is still coming up out of the cellar. The country once had lots of nice cycle paths. They were ripped up to make room for cars. It is taking a little while to get the space back, and cycle planners sometimes have to settle for what they can get. Bottom line: some cycle paths are intelligently designed and work; others are dangerous and best avoided.

4. Tracks, parks, canal towpaths, bridle paths and other byways. Once there were no cars! People went by foot and on horses and bicycles. It is absolutely amazing how many byways still exist. Many are legally open to cyclists, and greatly increase the range of possibilities for journeys. For example, London has a number of canals. You can drop down from

a street onto a canal path, ride for several miles utterly removed from the hustle and bustle of the city above, and then pop up near your destination.

Byways have amenity value. Some pass through industrial areas and can be rugged or littered, but many are verdant and peaceful. This means that other folks use them, too, and shared-use makes it incumbent upon cyclists to be well mannered and considerate. Even at a modest 8 MPH, a cyclist can come up fairly fast on someone walking their dog or strolling with a toddler, or lost contemplating butterflies. Cut everyone lots of slack. Keep it a nice world.

Regent's Canal, London

Parks are something of a special case. Some parks sensibly have cycle paths. Many parks are technically closed to cyclists, but no one fusses about people riding through. In a few, Old Bill is on the prowl, not for bank robbers or dope fiends, but for cyclists! Such anti-crime programmes are often caused by a few rogue cyclists misbehaving and scaring other park users. After a hue and cry, the problem passes.

The thing about parks is — shared-use! It is absolutely incumbent for cyclists to ride in such a way as to not spook or otherwise upset other park users. This includes pedestrians blithely walking along in cycle

Travel by train, bicycle or canal. Malmo, Sweden

paths. In this world, a bike is a HGV, and you need to take the initiative in ensuring that other people are comfortable with your presence. (I'll slip you some how-to tips in the riding section.)

5. Mixed-mode transport. Ah, back in the world of distance and speed! To reprise, mixed-mode means combining cycling with other transport,

including trains, buses, and cars, and boats, and sometimes even aircraft. There are two fundamental methods: use one bike and take it on whatever is the other mode, or use two bikes, one at each destination point.

There are a range of factors to take into account when setting up for mixed-mode transport. An obvious one is: does the alternate mode permit carriage of cycles? You have to check the specific situation. If there is a ban, you need to consider the two bike option, or a folding bike.

Variety

The chemistry and nature of a bike ride are going to depend on the purpose of the journey, and also on what you want out of it. For example, when shopping for groceries, you are unlikely to need to go far, or be interested in working up a lather. Poking along a cycle path is fine. On a 3-mile commute to work, you may want a tight, focused, cobweb-blowing ride. You'll want fast routes. On the other hand, rush hour is when motorists frenzy and become more aggressive; the pleasure and ease of cycling on a tranquil route such as a canal tow-path may be well worth a few minutes extra journey time. One fine advantage of cycling is that you have a choice, and can tailor your journey to suit your mood and needs.

Just the thing for a run to the shops . . .

Kinds of Cycles

For transport cycling, it is worth using a bike (or bikes) designed for your particular workaday tasks and lifestyle. If you dream of riding the Tour de France and your heart is set on having a lightweight road racing bike, that is a wonderful but separate affair. Sport and utility functions can sometimes be combined, but are usually best kept apart. Prioritise the working bike you use daily, and add others as fun and fancy take you. There is everything right with having three, four, five or even more bikes. Whatever else is life for?

Think about what you want to do, and explore possibilities with an open mind, as there are lots of new designs. 'Utility' does not necessarily mean slow or crude. In the past, working bikes were cheap and heavy; today, many designs positively sparkle with innovation and quality, and are a joy because they are both efficient and fun to use.

Roadster

Roadster bikes are designed to be comfortable and practical in everyday use. Universal characteristics are an upright riding position on a comfy saddle, flat or upswept handlebars, full-length mudguards, and a chain guard. Many models also include built-in lights, a rear parcel carrier, and a prop-stand. There are three general types.

Veteran, or Old Ironsides

Design ca. 1910, still in extensive use in the Netherlands and throughout Africa and Asia. Elegant and graceful in appearance but exceedingly heavy

(23 kg and more). A full chain guard completely encloses the chain so dirt cannot get in, which reduces maintenance to a minimum, and prevents staining of clothes. Basic, ancient-pattern machines have rod brakes, which are weak and unsafe. Contemporary models with hub brakes are reliable stoppers, but are still dreadnoughts. Great if you live in flat country. Otherwise, if you fancy the old-fashioned look, far better to seek out a modern art-nouveau design with a lightweight frame and modern components.

Veteran Roadster

Modern 'Old Ironsides' with all-weather hub brakes. A full chain guard ensures long chain life and clean clothes. The guard over the rear wheel helps stop a skirt or coat from tangling in the spokes. Majestic and stylish, but very heavy, and lots of hard work up hills.

Classic, or Norman Tebbit

Cabinet minister Norman Tebbit gained lasting fame when he advised the jobless to get 'On Yer Bike!' and seek work. Were it so simple. Norman's bite-the-bullet steed for vanquishing unemployment was likely a classic roadster, design ca. 1930, with a frame of inexpensive mild steel, steel wheels, three-speed hub gears, and cheap, unreliable side-pull calliper brakes. At 16 kg and up, still a heavy machine.

A classic roadster can be a useful local runabout, mainly because it has little appeal for theft. Best if the bike is beat-up and worn. Used, these machines change hands for little money, and I have rescued a number from the scrap heap for free. There is no point to buying one new; the cost is just as high as for a bike of better design and safer performance. Times have moved on.

Norman Tebbit Special (classic roadster) with 3-speed hub gears.

These prosaic machines do not excite thieves, hence need not be secured with three heavy-duty locks and a guard dog when parked. For safety, be mortally certain to fit modern all-weather brake shoes. Otherwise, a ride in wet conditions may pass through the Pearly Gates.

Modern Roadster

This category covers a wide range of well-made models equipped with quality components that perform properly. You get what you pay for. At the bottom end, the bikes are still fairly heavy; at the top end, they are made from lightweight materials and sport all sorts of nifty features — high-performance brakes, slathers of gears, and a range of accoutrements designed to make your life easier.

Robust, modern roadster

A modern roadster can capably manage mid-range commuting journeys, and extend to more distant runs and tours if it is a good model and you are comfortable on it. A really sparkling modern roadster is second to none in quality (or price!). Many use hub gears, which reduces maintenance, and makes it easier to fit a chain guard. You can ride wearing ordinary clothes. Brakes are at least V-calliper, and often are hub-type, which perform more consistently in wet weather. The main point is that the machines are designed for urban use.

Mountain Bike

Or "bicycle". Definitely the most universal of cycles, able to negotiate mountain tracks and high streets with equal ease. Best to get a few points straight, though.

Prices range from under £60 in supermarkets to over £3000 in bike shops. Cheap supermarket models are not going to scale Kilimanjaro and might even flounder on a run through a golf course. Ballpark, think around £325 for an entry-level mountain bike which can go off-road for real and come back in one piece, and around £225 for a machine that will do nicely enough on the street, and manage off-road forays so long as the going is not rough.

Mountain Bike — Condor Cadenza

A rigid (no suspension) mountain bike. Simple and tough, and a great all-round machine.

Street hardtail

Suspension forks ease road shock on hands and arms; hardtail rear transmits power without up-and-down 'bobbing'.

There is more — oh yes! Around £500 puts you in the way of some really nice bikes, and around £1000 and up can perch you on a machine which will make you chirp and sing. Going (affordably) upmarket is well worth the money, but beware feature overload. Mountain bikes benefit from very evolved technology, most notably in the area of suspension. Some people make the error of trying to 'get' as many hi-tech features as possible. Don't. Concentrate on essential quality (light weight and good components) first, and hi-tech features second.

If you are a keen off-road rider, a mountain bike can be a true dual-purpose machine: a swift weekday commuter, and a rugged weekend off-road sport/touring vehicle. The trick is done by running two sets of wheels, one with fast road tyres, the other with dirt tyres. On commutes it is the fast wheels plus clip-on mudguards. Off-road it is the dirt-pluggers (and you might still want the mudguards).

Condor Bivio

Nice hybrid, suitable for running two sets of wheels.

Mountain bikes are justifiably popular for urban use. They are tough, adaptable, quick when set up correctly, and lots and lots and lots of fun.

Downhill Mountain Bike

Interested in off-road downhill racing, on a bike with elaborate, sexy, deep-travel suspension? Great! But that's sport; the bikes are too heavy for everyday riding.

Hybrid

Hybrid bikes are designed for street use and light off-road riding, such as along bridle paths, canal tow paths, and smooth tracks. Some hybrids are essentially mountain bike designs re-tuned for street use, often with slightly larger 700 wheels and narrower, harder tyres. Some models include roadster conveniences such as mudguards, chain guard, and parcel rack, and perhaps lights and a prop-stand. Hybrids roll along smoothly, yet can stand moderately rough going. They can be fine long-distance commuting and touring machines.

Sherry's Condor Hybrid

Sherry's city/sport bike has about the smallest frame possible with full-size 700C wheels. Lightweight and easy-rolling, yet tough, this is one of the best bikes in the family stable.

Condor Strada

Fast commuter road bike.

City Bike

City bikes are pretty much like hybrids, but are expressly designed for urban cycling. The differences are subtle, but real. Hybrid bikes look toward sport, and tend to be slightly lean; city bikes are purpose-specific, and tend to be a bit more robust, and more eclectic in selection of components. A quintessential city bike might have strong wheels with wide, smooth tyres, full length mudguards, chain guard, stout parcel/pannier carrier, built-in lights, and other mod cons. Again, you-get-what-you-pay-for applies, and cheaper models are heavier and not as sprightly and as much fun as the more expensive and lighter models. City bikes are just fine for everyday riding and long commuting journeys. If well-made they can also venture off-road.

City Bike

SUSPENSION?

Suspension for bikes ranges from complex mechanisms designed to absorb major impacts, to simple devices designed to reduce the sting of bumps. Full-on suspension systems add weight, and can lead to 'bobble' while pedalling; energy wasted in up and down motion. Rear suspension is over the top for urban riding. Front suspension may make riding rough streets easier, but there is a price in weight, and increased maintenance.

Personally, I prefer simpler touches. Inflating tyres to the right pressure for your weight has a big effect on comfort. (For particulars, see the Maintenance chapter, p.235-238.) Gel-filled gloves are nice, and wrapping the bars with quality foam helps. Some saddles are designed for a small amount of shock absorption. Another option are shock-absorbing seat posts.

Road racing or Sport

Road racing bikes with drop handlebars are designed with pretty much just one idea in mind: to be wings for the feet. Conditioned club riders average 18 to 19 MPH on the open road, and do 100-mile rides with comparative ease.

Real road racing bikes are not found in grocery stores. They combine light weight with strength, i.e. are made with quality materials, and as with real mountain bikes, cost a bit of lolly. Still, you can snag a good entry-level road bike for a surprisingly reasonable sum, and perhaps should do so — as a sport. I do not recommend road racing bikes for regular urban riding, as to survive mean streets they need a peculiar mixture of TLC and athletic bike handling skills. On the other hand, if you have a long commuting journey and want to take a sport bonus, a road racing bike is motion incarnate.

Condor Italia

Touring

A classic touring bike is built strong and stiff, to maintain stability when laden with heavy baggage. Typically, panniers are hung fore and aft, for a balanced load. This arrangement is fine for self-contained long-distance tours, but is not so good for urban living. Managing groceries and other of life's sundries on and off a touring bike is a never-ending juggle of panniers and straps and buckles, and none of this stuff can be left behind if you lock up on the street. There are easier ways!

Full-on touring bike

Fixed Wheel

Hang out where bike couriers congregate, and you are sure to spot the greyhounds of the cycling world: very lightweight frames set up as single-speed with a fixed wheel. There is just one front chain ring and one sprocket on the rear, which does not freewheel; when the cranks turn, the rear wheel turns, and vice-versa. One front brake (back-pedal to brake the rear wheel). This set-up is as simple and minimalist as can be, and is all about light weight and highly tuned riding skills. The people who can handle these bikes are very, very good. As an ambition — great.

Condor Fisso

Lightweight street bike that can be fitted with a reversible rear wheel; on one side, the freewheel is fixed, on the other, the freewheel is free.

More practical for town use is a single-speed with a freewheel and brakes front and rear. This sort of bike is lightweight, strong, and simple, and very effective as personal transport. Using just one gear is Spartan, but good for you. You've got to ride, and of needs, you become more supple and skilled. For a day-in day-out transport bike that is simple to use and service, and lightweight enough to be easily handled, a single-speed is an option well worth considering. (Have another bike, with gears, for hauling groceries and attempts on Everest.)

As a matter of interest, my current town bike is a single-speed. It is made of carbon fibre and weighs a flat 10 kg!

2D Town Bike by Mike Burrows

Hand-made prototype. This design could be mass-produced at low cost and would be ideal for fleet sales to companies.

The wheels are 20-inch, the brakes are hub, and the fully enclosed chain guard also mounts the rear wheel. The machine is ultra-low maintenance: the chain needs oil once a year, the brakes need attention every two years. It is a fine town bike. The ride is smooth, the handling sure and confident, and the bike is a breeze to carry up and down stairs when using trains.

Cargo and Freight Cycles

At the rear of our garden shed reposes an ancient delivery bike souped up as a hot-rod with derailleur gears. I used to take it out to the park and spring surprises on Sunday racers. It is also heavy and strong enough to have real authority in an argument with a car. I guess bike builders of yore figured that since delivery bikes would be hauling loads, they might as well be made of very heavy tubing.

Times have moved on — and how! Modern cargo bikes are an evolved and extraordinarily useful species, available in a range of different designs to suit different purposes. Some are even rather nice for touring. Many are made in lightweight materials and fitted with high-performance components.

Christiana

One classic utility model is the box tricycle, with the rider pushing a platform, box, or enclosed cabin for children. Box trikes are great for ferrying kids to school, and hauling around groceries and gardening and building supplies. They are slow and steady rather than quick or deft, and are more comfortable to use on quiet streets and cycle paths than on main routes thick with fast-moving motor vehicles.

Another type of tricycle, popular for use as a pedi-cab, places the rider in front. At the rear, there is a platform, or a big box, or a set-up for seating passengers. I was surprised the first time I tried one of these with two big fellows as passengers. Once up to speed, maintaining momentum is not such hard work — on flat ground. Hills are another story, and a worthwhile option is electric assist. A push of a button engages an electric motor that gives a boost when starting away from stop, or climbing. The electric assist is designed for power, not speed, so you get help when you really need it, but otherwise, you pedal. This kind of a set-up is neigh-ideal for local transport, shopping, and light trades such as carpentry and interior decorating. Capital cost is high — say £3000 — but there is no road tax or insurance, and parking anywhere at any time is free. You can treat yourself to a 'number plate' with a rude insult for parking wardens.

Cycles Maximus

Robust trike that can variously be set up an open cargo carrier, enclosed box van, or pedi-cab. It was developed in Bath, where the hills are steep, and has electric-assist as an option.

The cargo bike I saved my pennies to buy is the 8-Freight, designed by Mike Burrows. This one is a dilly. It is a tandem-size bicycle without a rear seat. Instead, behind the rider there is large, low-slung cargo area that can be filled with a big basket or box. A strong platform over the rear wheel gives an extra load area, and works fine as seat for a passenger. At the front, a quick-release basket is a handy hold-all.

Sunny's Ride

Danielle and Sunny checking out our new 8-Freight.

The 8-Freight is made from aluminium and has modern components. The design has two big advantages. The cargo area is low down, so heavy loads have little adverse effect on bike handling. And the machine is a proper bike that is easy to manage in traffic. In fact, once you get used to the long wheelbase, the bike has an odd carefree charm. It's quite fun to ride, and soon becomes the mount of choice for little errands and jaunts, as well as more robust freight-hauling chores. It is also a brilliant machine for heavily-laden cycle camping.

There are loads more specialised cargo designs, for example, bikes set up with a child seat at the front or rear, and a baggage area at the opposite end. Others have features such as a child seat that can double as a pram. Two excellent publications/web sites packed with information are Encyclopedia and VeloVision.

The drawback of large cargo cycles is their size. These are not machines to wrestle up and down stairs, or stash in a hallway. You need accessible outside parking, such as in a forecourt or garden, shed, or covered alley. Perhaps in a neighbour's garage. More on this in the section on Parking, p.133.

Working vehicles

Folding Bikes

Folding bikes are exploding in popularity. Two reasons: mixed-mode transport and security. Britain's train services have become increasingly unfriendly to bikes and many prohibit them at commuting times. Folders are immune to bans and make mixed-mode transport practical. Folders also obviate need for carrying a battery of heavy locks. A folder can go into places of work, restaurants, etc. and is easy to keep somewhere in a house or flat. This huge reduction in the problem of theft is a major asset, especially for someone who lives where the only secure parking is inside their residence.

There is a rub or two, of course. Devising a folding bike that rides well, yet easily reduces to a compact, manageable package, is the holy grail of cycle designers. Meeting both criteria at once is exceedingly difficult, and few have succeeded. Most folding bikes compromise to one degree or another on weight, ease and compactness of folding, and ride performance. What is suitable depends on application. A folder for a car boot need only ride well and reduce in size; it does not matter if the machine is too heavy and awkward to manage on a train. One thing to be clear about: an 'umbrella' bicycle that can be folded or unfolded by anyone in a snap, has not to my knowledge ever been attained in worthwhile form. Good folders are specialised machines, and to get the

Sinclair A-bike

Lightweight, wonderfully compact, and totally unsafe. The small wheels on Sir Sinclair's bike guarantee a wipe-out, if the rider is not first hammered to jelly by the rough ride.

most out of using one, you need to enjoy being deft and clever about managing bits and pieces, and either have a strong arm or a deep wallet.

The legendary Brompton marque sets the benchmark for good compactness and ride performance. The old standard model weighs nearly 16 kg (about 35 lb.), which is grunt-hefty, but the new lightweight range includes a model with titanium bits that weighs under 9.7 kg (21 lb.)! At around £1000 the machine is expensive, but the light weight makes a sensational difference to ease of handling when folded. The folding sequence is precise, but quick. The Brompton is expressly designed for mixed-mode transport. It is the only folding bike that can be viably accessorised to carry luggage.

Airnimal bikes are upmarket machines providing road performance at the same level as standard-size bikes. I had a spin on one recently and was thoroughly impressed; lightweight, sweet-handling, and responsive. Airnimal bikes are about clever engineering; some models will fold and disassemble to fit into a suitcase. The process takes time,

Brompton

though. These machines are great for travellers who want a fine bike while on holiday or extended trips. They are not suitable for commuters rushing for a train.

Airnimal

A folder deserves very serious consideration for urban transport, but be prepared to spend £500 for a basic model, and up to £2000 for something really fancy. Cheap folders are heavy and/or awkward when folded, or, if lightweight, ride miserably and fold poorly. The exact point of a folding bike is that it works at least acceptably as a bike, and folds quickly into an easily managed package. This is the key to success with mixed-mode transport, and to having a machine which you can easily check into a cloakroom, or pop into a taxi-cab on a monsoon day.

If you want a folder which only has to go into a car boot or downstairs closet, then the current tip for best value and performance tip is a Hon. The bike has fairly large wheels and rides well, and is keenly priced at around £300. Another good ride model is the Giant Half-way.

For the latest info and a good guide to folding bikes, go to http://www. atob.org.uk and click on Buyer's Guide.

Laid Back

Do it lying down! Laid back (nee recumbent) cycles are fast, comfortable, and, in comparison to upright bikes, have more powerful braking capacity and greater safety. Laid back cycles are about speed. On an upright bike at 20 MPH, around 80 per cent of the rider's energy output goes into pushing through the air. A recumbent configuration reduces aerodynamic drag, and basically, the more laid back the machine and the smaller the frontal area, the faster it can be made to go.

Laid back cycles are at their best on the open road, where they can stretch out and go. They are good for long commuting runs, but the speed is not much use in dense traffic, or for short journeys. However, the riding position is super-comfortable, and this factor can be very important for people who are prone to sore hands, backs, or bums, when riding upright bikes.

Many people are wary of laid back cycles, imagining they must be unsafe because they are hard to see. This is not the case. However, some designs are better for traffic than others. Here is a brief run-down on types.

Easy Rider

The laid back equivalent of a roadster is an easy rider, where the rider sits fairly high up and the bottom bracket is lower than the rider's hips. The rider can easily touch feet to ground, and does not have far to go when lifting a foot to the pedal. An easy rider has no aerodynamic advantage over an upright bike. The virtues are easy handling, plenty of comfort, and better braking. The high seat gives the rider a good view of traffic. An easy rider is fine as a neighbourhood runabout, and for short- and medium-distance commuting. It is good as a first recumbent for learning.

HP Spirit — comfortable easy rider

Touring and Sport

Touring and sport laid back bikes typically have a lower and more recumbent riding position, with the bottom bracket near to the level of the rider's hips. Many machines include a tail box or boot. These help improve aerodynamic efficiency, and give a place to carry gear, a few groceries, or whatever. Initial rides on these machines may be awkward. It takes a little while to pick up the skills that enable confident bike handling. These machines can be demanding to manage in stop-and-go traffic.

HP Street Machine

A touring model that is stable and easy to manage, but heavy and hence a bit of work in dense traffic.

Rat 9 by Mike Burrows

A lightweight (12 kg), fast bike with quick handling. Intended for fast day riding and best suited to the open road, but experienced riders can manage heavy traffic. The tail fairing is also a large boot.

RACING

All-out racing recumbent bikes streamline the rider configuration as much as possible. Some are so low-down, you have to bend over to look at them. Others use big wheels and lift the rider up fairly high. Either way, racing recumbent bikes are not for runs to the shops. They are very, very fast, and handling is sometimes challenging.

Denise Wilson/Rat Racer at CycleVision

Trikes

A laid back tricycle is rather special. A low centre of gravity makes the machine stable, yet incredibly quick and agile. In fact, few things in life are so exciting as letting it all hang out on a well designed laid back trike. And yet, in thick stop-and-go traffic one can just laze along in armchair comfort, poking the pedals now and again when necessary.

Speedy!

The down side? Trikes are big. In heavy traffic, you cannot squeeze through gaps as easily as on a bike. At home, finding a parking space may involve careful choreography. Hence, while my Windcheetah SL 'Speedy' tricycle is much-used and much-loved, for riding around town, most often I use either my work bike, a custom-design with a huge rear rack, or the ultra-light and simple 2D. Bikes are just so easy. Still, if I were to have just one machine, I would stand by my Speedy.

Opposite: Line-up at CycleVision

Velomobiles can be practical for transport, but there are catches, of course. The human engine must dissipate as heat four to five units of energy for every unit of energy put into the pedals. Since the power plant is air-cooled, it is prone to over-heat when inside a full fairing. A velomobile is a treat on a cold day, but in mild or warm conditions, an open or part-faired HPV is more comfortable. Another snag: a velomobile is too large to pop into the house. Unless you have a garage or large bike port, it has to live outside, on the street or in a front yard.

VELOMOBILE

A velomobile is a special machine: a laid back cycle with a full or partial fairing, set up for use on the street. Most are trikes. Reason: full-faired HPVs are vulnerable to cross-winds and turbulence from other vehicles. Trikes are usually manageable, but bikes can veer out of control. The latter are only for well-experienced HPV riders.

Velomobiles are fast but heavy, hence at their best on open roads. I used a velomobile for commuting in London for many years, with great success. It was swift, exciting, comfy when the weather was foul, and safe. However, my machine weighed about 22 kg; current models go 35 kg and higher. Velomobiles are popular in the Netherlands, where the flat terrain, extensive cycle path network, and often windy and wet weather, make such machines practical. They have some very beautiful designs!

FWD Cafe Racer — Mike Burrows

Ask for 'Alfie'! Cafe racer/Sunday special/ fun machine. Tech-exotic front wheel drive, but the handling is surprisingly easy.

II:WHEEL DEALING

Finance

Cycling is economical. If you have income or capital, investment in a bike will quickly be recouped. If you are broke or without any spare change, do what you can afford, and upgrade when times are better. You can promote a bike for a few quid, or even for free. The machine might be a bit rough, but will get you started.

At the other end of the spectrum, you can splurge for the most exotic, refined bike in the country, and still spend less than the price of cheap car. If you hanker for a machine costing a few thousand pounds and can afford it, then treat yourself!

Credit

Credit is OK if the savings from using a bike will be greater than the cost of borrowing. Shop around. Banks and credit card companies are expensive, and pull tricks. Many bike shops give credit. But see below!

Bikes Half-price, On the Drip, No Interest Charge!

If you are waged, it is possible to purchase a bike, plus accessories such as locks, lights, clothes, helmets, and any other necessary equipment, at little more than half the normal price, on credit with no interest charge! The scheme is promoted by the Inland Revenue and here is how this sweetheart deal works.

Your employer pays the cost of the bike and bits, and recovers by deducting instalments from your wages over 12 or 18 months. You pay no tax or National Insurance on the repayments, and after VAT rebates and other discounts are taken into account, your all-up cost is a bit more than half of what you would have spent if you had gone to the shop and paid yourself.

You have to say you will use the bike only for riding to and from work, and the machine has to be an adult model. Help for employers in implementing the scheme is provided by an independent organisation, Booost (01582 406111 or http://www.booost.uk.com). Full details in the Inland Revenue Green Travel Plan IR176 leaflet, available from their website http://www. hmrc.gov.uk.

The incentive for employers is simple: a happier, healthier, more productive and more loyal work force. Employees who cycle to work take fewer sick days, work harder, and stay in employment for longer. Get this scheme going at your place of work and you will score points for helping your employer's business, do genuine good all around, and score a bike!

Customised 8-Freight used by a photo equipment rental firm for deliveries in London. The bike cost less than the annual congestion charge on a motor vehicle, and is often faster, too! The long tubes are for viewing screens.

Self-employed

If you are self-employed, transport costs in conducting your business are tax-deductible. For cycling this involves both capital depreciation, and mileage allowances. Check with the Inland Revenue for guidelines.

Insurance

I hate betting on the loss of a bike. But a disaster or theft could happen, and if you cannot afford the loss, then consider having insurance. If you have a household policy, check the terms as many cover pedal cycles, or have all risks cover available for an extra premium. Bike-specific policies are available through cyclists groups and bike shops. Cycleguard is supported by the Association of Cycle Traders (www.cycleguard.co.uk). Whichever firm or organisation you try, ask for satisfied-customer recommendations, and watch the wording on new-for-old and depreciation clauses. Gambling casinos and insurance companies are in business to take your money, not give you theirs.

Lock city

The £0 Bicycle or Red Saddles Are Free

The Old Spokes Home

In Woodstock, New York, people take old and unwanted bikes to the Old Spokes Home. The proprietor, Mike Esposito, a preacher and evangelist cyclist, cannibalises and recycles the machines into working bikes, paints the saddles red, and leaves them around town for people to use for free.

Saint Michael

Mike is riding an old JC Higgins.

You, too, can have a bike for free!

Bikes are regularly abandoned on the street, tossed into skips, and left to rot in alleyways and behind hedges. I have a scavenger's eye for such things, but still, it is amazing how many bikes are just discarded. Usually, they evince symptoms of neglect: flat tyres, broken cables, rusty chains, busted spokes, twisted bits, etc. Some are well and truly scrap. Others are only in poor running order, or have but one serious defect. Take two, three, or four of these, pick and choose the best bits, do a bit of greasy shuffle and voila – a running bicycle!

An excellent source of materials are recycling centres. I've seen mounds of discarded bikes! Make friends with the recycling people, and they will probably let you pick and choose on the spot. This saves lugging a lot of junk home.

A bike?

It is best to follow a theme. For example, 20 and 30 years ago, a type of bike known as a ten-speed was popular. These are now steadily migrating from sheds and attics to skips and dumps. For some, new parts are no longer available – not a problem if you have a half-dozen machines to pick from.

Roadsters are another staple. I can still see a sweet 1952 ladies Triumph that I found at the dump, and fixed up, two-tone paint job and all. Can't remember what I did with it. (I'm a bit of a Johnny Appleseed with bikes.)

Mountain bikes are frequently discarded, but are usually cheap, low-end machines. These can be difficult to work with. If you want to create a re-cycled mountain bike, then be prepared to search and pick for bits over some time. Old small-wheel 'shopper' bikes turn up fairly often, but, with few exceptions, are not worth restoring.

Down And Greasy

How do you recycle a bike? You've got to learn! This is part of the fun and value to you of the whole enterprise. Build a bike or two and you will never want for transport again.

First stop: a library. I am a great one for starting mechanical and building projects by soaking up what my Dad always called "The book of the words." There are plenty of good repair and how-to-do-it manuals for bikes. Get a selection, and read them again and again until you know how a bike works.

Not a reader? Got to go hands-on? Then make friends with someone who knows enough to be able to help out and give advice. Such people are there, you have to ask — and the old saying 'see, ask and you shall be given,' is true. Try your local community centre and/or cycle campaign group, for courses in bike maintenance. Or join a barter group such as LETS and see if you can trade for help working on a bike.

You will need some basic tools. Beg and borrow and no pinching, eh? Steal a tool, might as well steal a bike. It's not what we are about. For borrowing, ask nicely, and you might be surprised at how many people will help out. Remember, you are doing a Good Thing. Be faithful about returning borrowed tools. For low-budget tools, cost in pence not pounds, check out car boot sales, garage sales, and similar. For oil, rummage in the waste at a petrol station. For grease, ask an auto mechanic to give you a shot in a plastic bag or cup; it will be plenty enough for a bike. Also scrounge some paint thinner or penetrating oil, to help undo rust-frozen parts.

General Principles & Tips

»   The frame must be reasonably sound. Surface rust is not a problem, but if part of the frame is damaged or seriously bent, find another. Especially check that the forks have not been bent.

Paint wrinkles indicate crash damage

» Unless you are lucky, finding good wheels will take some hunting. A wheel is an engineering structure that can be knocked out of shape or damaged beyond repair or restoration. Look and look again. Extra effort here will be amply repaid.

» Bearings that are stiff may still not be too worn; bearings that are very loose or rough may be past redemption.

» Simplify. If you are working with a derailleur gear bike and the changers are shot, you can make the machine a single-speed. Simply shorten the chain to fit over whatever front chain ring/rear cog combination gives you a comfortable gear. Upgrade later, when you find another bike with transmission bits in good condition.

Advanced DIY class: custom street bikes

Bikes £0 to £400 and More

£0 to £25

Buy a bike for £10 or £15? Sure enough. There are quite a few ways of turning this trick. Keep a watch on ads in local newspapers and in newsagents' windows. At the start of summer, school notice-boards fill with offers of bikes and other gear. You might get lucky at a car boot or garage sale. Remember, asking price is not necessarily selling price. It is fine to offer what you can afford, even if it is less than a bike is worth. In the absence of a better offer, the seller may be happy to take your money.

How much for the lot?

Scout around your patch. Where there are sheds and gardens, there are bikes. Right in the forecourt of a house near mine, there are a half-dozen mountain bikes that have not moved in at least two or three years. I could probably have the lot for £20. Try putting up notices around the neighbourhood:

Old Bike Wanted

Got an unwanted bike in your garden or shed? I

need a bike for transport. Anything considered.

Ring Richard on 01234 567 890

For up to £25, expect a running roadster or an ancient 10-speed in need of attention. If lucky, you might find an old mountain bike that still has miles left to go.

£25 to £50

The start of serious money, and dangerous territory, too. Bikes in this price range can be mechanically pretty desperate. A roadster or old 10-speed should be in good condition. With a mountain bike, be sure you know what you are doing! It would be luck indeed to find a decent mountain bike for under £50.

Private sales are your best bet. *Loot* and E-bay have bikes at under £50, but again, watch out for condition. Be aware: adverts in local newspapers are sometimes by traders. In some cases the provenance of the bike may be dubious. Use common sense and stay away from deals that look dodgy.

Falcon Lady's Lightweight, 531 tubing, 21in frame, 10-speed, 27 x 1¼ alloy wheels, alloy straight "all-rounder" h/bars, mudguards, centre pull brakes, black finish £50

Ad from News & Views, newsletter of the Veteran Cycle Club. The bike is a quality lightweight, and if in good condition, a snip at £50.

Street markets are, alas, often outlets for stolen bikes. Yet street markets are fun, and sensible as a low-overhead venue for low-cost bikes. Go with what feels right. Local markets with regular vendors might be OK. Big, well-known street markets are one of the first places to look when a bike has been nicked. But these places have honest traders, too.

One prize source of cheap bikes are police auctions. Few of the bikes recovered by the police are claimed by their owners, so from time to time they hold auctions. As you might expect, buyers sometimes ride off on real bargains. If you go to one of these, be patient. The pattern is for bidding to be brisk on early lots, then settle down.

£50 to £100

Basically, for £0 to £50 you can be happy with a bike that simply works; for £50 to £100 you can hope for a bike that will work fairly well, or even very well. Problem: lots of people are up for having a decent bike at £100, so such machines are rarely available for long.

Some bike shops have used machines, but any bike priced at £100 or less that is worth having will roll out quickly. Private sales are your best bet. An ideal find would be, say, a bike purchased new three or four years ago for £250 to £300. The owner wanted the bike for commuting or Sunday rides or whatever, but as matters worked out, the bike was little-used and has less than 2000 miles of wear. Eureka! With luck, you might also score a decent lock and perhaps a helmet, too. Remember, "but it was £250 new!" doesn't hack it. £100 or a squeeze more for such a bike is better than what the owner will realise flogging the bike to a shop or street trader.

Watch condition! New consumables (tyres, cables, chain) can easily run another £100. It depends on the details. For example, with a cable, if only the wire needs replacing, the expense is not bad; however, if the housing is also gone, so is enough change for a modest meal. Major components such as crank sets and wheels can be right expensive. Remember, the cheapest way to buy new components is to buy a new bike, as just the components alone will cost more! Still, let's say you find a really rather nice bike that originally cost £350, with a pranged front wheel. You offer £100, reckoning on £25 to £50 for a new wheel.

When shopping for used bikes, you need to be able to accurately suss out the condition of the machine, and what any repairs are likely to cost.

This usually means enlisting the help of a knowledgeable friend. If you have such a person on tap, lucky you . . . and I suggest resource conservation. Organise a shopping/buying expedition so that in an afternoon, you look at 3 or 4 machines; chances are you will score well enough on one of them.

Being able to chat to people and draw them out can be useful. Always ask about the history of a bike, and look for a straight story. On the other hand, do not bet the farm just because the vendor seems to be an OK person.

£100 to £200

The start of interesting territory. With a bit of luck (and ready hard cash) you might find a new bike that is genuinely lightweight, with reasonable-quality components. Look for closeout sales, when shops dispose of old stocks and odd machines. Some shops specialise in clearance sales of last years' models. There are bargains to be had, but check mechanical condition carefully.

Used can be exciting, because this is where you begin to find full-on, serious bikes that originally cost £500 and up. You can also be taken for a ride! Bikes in this price range are often worn-out, hurt, or hot — stolen.

Sources: bike shops, sure, but don't blink; good, usable bikes in this price range move out fast. An advantage is that the shop should back up the machine; if they say "As is," then pass. Street traders, of course, but for goodness' sake, be sure the vibes feel straight and honest. *Loot*, E-bay, and other national publications, sure. Inside tip: check out bike magazines and club newsletters.

Ridgeback Genesis Day 0/0 hybrid, large frame, 1 year old, used for London-Southend bike ride only. Immaculate £160.

Carlton Corsair 23½" Reynolds 531 tubing frame 27" wheels 10 gears. Bronze and chrome. £120.

By now, you will be looking for fairly specific type of machine; a hybrid, say, or a go-for-it mountain bike. Condition is important. You've boned up on bike lore, and you have your handy knowledgeable friend in tow, too. No? Think a hybrid is a rose, and your friends are all into beer labels? OK, here is a trick to try.

22" Claud Butler Urban 200 hybrid brushed alu frame. As new, extras £200 ono. Welshpool

Claud Butler urban 200 hybrid AL 7005 alloyseries, Shimano Acera 21 gear, 2 years old very good condition, many extras, sell £125.
(Somerset)

Shop around

Scout out a bike shop in the area where you will be looking at a used bike. Ask the shop if they will give you a professional evaluation of a prospective used bike for, say, £10. Say that if the bike is OK, the £10 is theirs, and if the bike needs work, you would like the £10 credited toward the cost of the job. You might get a no. Not all bike shops are gifts from the Almighty. But you might well get a good response, perhaps something like: 'Well, OK on a weekday but not on Saturdays.'

Then, for a bike you like, agree with the vendor to buy subject to survey. The seller brings the bike to the shop at a specified time (then and there is best), and if the shop gives it a clean bill of health, you do

Specialized Hardrock XC, mint condition, only used twice, silver and black, 17in frame, 24spd, also included: Blackburn mini pump, lock, tube and puncture outfit (never used) £170. Tel (Dumfries).

the deal at the agreed price. If the bike needs work, you can re-negotiate price. This process often goes more smoothly when an outside, third party has supplied the valuation.

£200 to £400

Firmly into new bike country now. For around £250 to £275 (less, with luck) you can have a new bike that is a genuine lightweight with decent components. A machine of this grade is fine for commuting, local use, and occasional jaunts and tours. For around £350 you can get a new bike which will last as well as any other; spend more, and you either get less weight and more performance (example, a carbon-fibre frame), or more in the way of features and technological wizardry (example, disc brakes instead of V-brakes).

Benchmark a new quality lightweight bike at £350, and buying used, the same money could catch a bike that originally cost as much as £700. You need serious luck to find a near-new bike in good condition at half price; more readily available are bikes one or two years old, at 75 per cent of original cost. On £350, that is a £500 original-price bike, which includes some pretty good machines. (And hey, if someone says 'It cost £800 new' — check that this was the real street price, and not the manufacturer's wished-for price.)

Whether you buy new or used is down to two factors: your budget, and your nature. If you have limited means and yearn for a fine performance bike or a bit of specialised iron (such as a fancy folder), or simply want best value, then buying used is the route to go. Pay attention and a fair price and things will probably go OK. If you just want to plunk down your boodle and have what you want, signed, sealed and delivered, then buy new.

Secrets of the Ancients - II

A while back, when discussing free recycled bikes, I pointed to classic 10-speeds of the 1970s and 1980s. There are literally millions gathering dust in sheds and attics. A properly overhauled 10-speed works perfectly well, even if the performance level is not as good as a modern machine. I usually give a little wolf whistle when I spot a clean old Peugeot UO-8, especially if it has a Huret Allvit derailleur (reverse charm, as it was the absolute worst ever made).

Jack Kirk (Hull) bicycle c1950s 22in frame, green with orange contrasts, half chrome forks and stays. Weinmann 27 x 1 /, 32/40. TA alloy double, steel cranks. Campag Gran Turismo rear, Benelux front. GB stem, Mafac brakes. Bluemels guards. Detailed specification on request and link to web photos. £85 ono.

Southampton

OK, here is another inside tip: quality classics. For £200 to £400 you can ride bikes that 20 to 40 years ago were the best around: marquees such as Mercian, Condor, Taylor, Holdsworthy, Evans, Quinn, Hall, and other famous names. Frames were hand-built, and the specification (component selection) was usually top-line: Campagnolo, Zeus, Stronglight, TA, and (later) Shimano Dura-Ace. These bikes have old-fashioned features, such as gear shift levers on the down tube, but are still performance thoroughbreds and a treat to ride.

We are talking road racing and touring models (mountain bikes only came on stream in the 1980s), and are now moving through a part of bike country where love is more important than money. Quality classics are owned and looked after by people who love cycling and have a thing for old bikes. As a result, vendors often prioritise moving a bike to a good home over how much money they get for it.

Of course there are sharpies, too, and you need to be technically capable, or have the help of a knowledgeable friend. A blown (frame dead from hard use) or clapped-out (components exhausted) classic is not an easy or quick repair. The best source, far and away, are the classified in *News and Views*, the quarterly newsletter of the Veteran Cycle Club. Ads for classics also sometimes appear in the CTC *Cycle* magazine, and in mainstream magazines such as *Cycling Plus*.

A quality classic is not a machine for a run to the shops. On the other hand, if you already have a transport/work bike, and are looking for a fun bike for Sunday rides and a turn of class worth spit and polish, then a classic can do nicely.

Story: one of my long-term ambitions was to have a Hetchins with curly chain stays, ruby red for a preference. This famous and distinctive marque commands high prices, and when one came up in the far north of England, I got aboard a train and rode a couple of hundred miles to go see it.

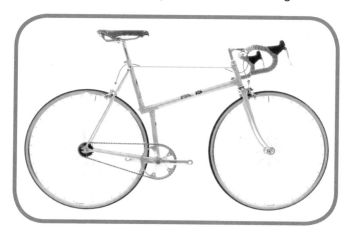

Condor Paris-Galibier

Modern version of a classic. Distinctive frame designs could be easily recognised when pictures of winning racers were published in the press.

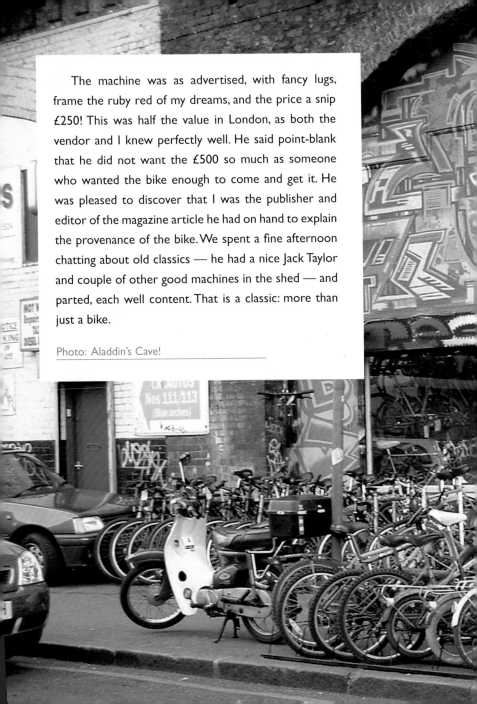

The machine was as advertised, with fancy lugs, frame the ruby red of my dreams, and the price a snip £250! This was half the value in London, as both the vendor and I knew perfectly well. He said point-blank that he did not want the £500 so much as someone who wanted the bike enough to come and get it. He was pleased to discover that I was the publisher and editor of the magazine article he had on hand to explain the provenance of the bike. We spent a fine afternoon chatting about old classics — he had a nice Jack Taylor and couple of other good machines in the shed — and parted, each well content. That is a classic: more than just a bike.

Photo: Aladdin's Cave!

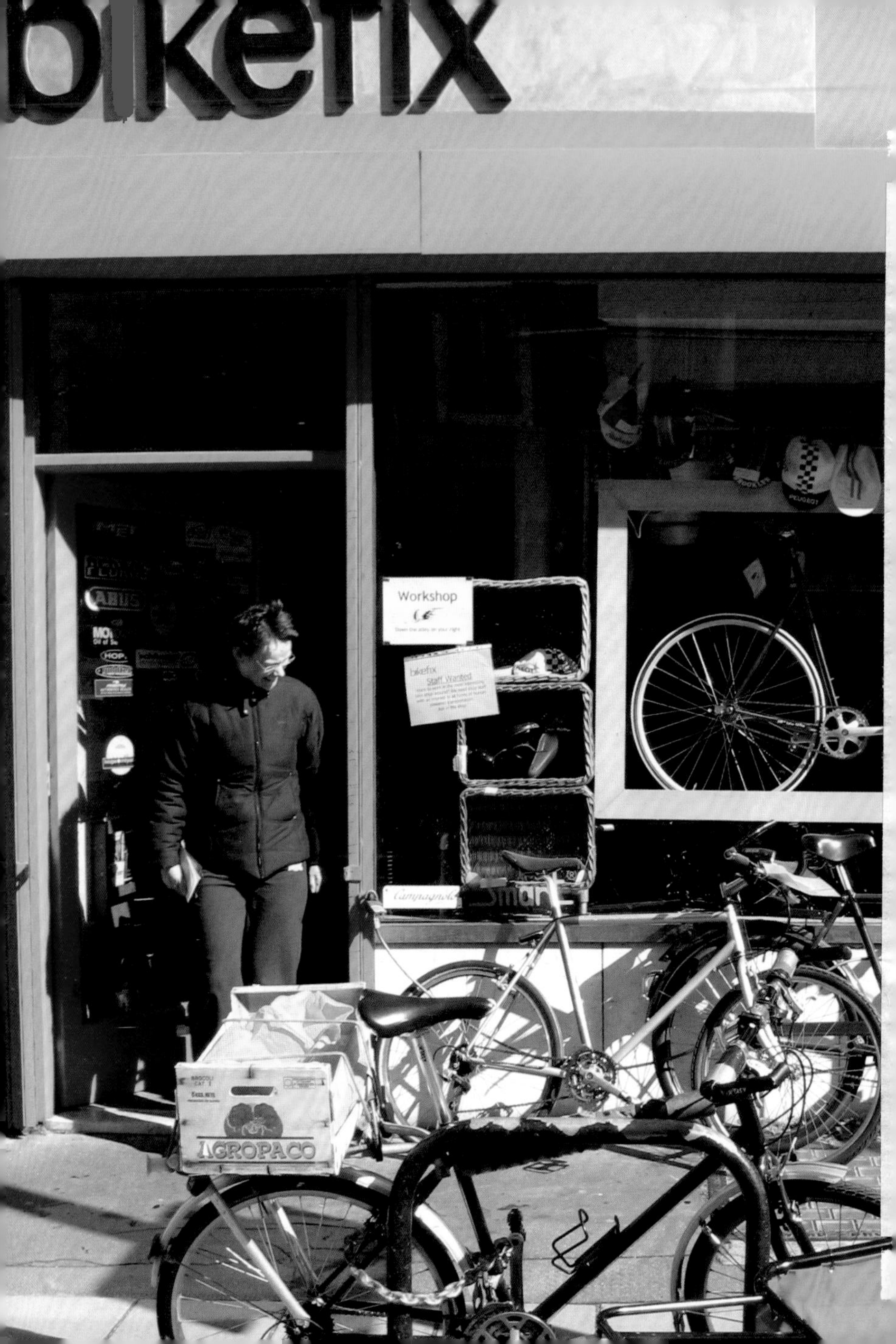
bikefix
Workshop
AGROPACO
Campagnolo

How To Buy A Bike

We're off to buy a bike! What do you look for, where do you look, and how do you get the best deal?

First, be as clear as possible about what you want. Fine to cruise a shop or two to see what is going, but efficient hunting means defining your requirements. This includes your budget.

New or used? Briefly, buying new from a shop, you should be guided to a bike that meets your needs and which works. Any problems, the shop should sort them. Buying used, you can hope to realise optimum value for money, but are on your own; any problems, you sort them. There are pros and cons both ways, and as well, your own nature is a factor. If you are a pay and go type, a shop may be best; if you enjoy hands-on mechanics, buying used may be the most rewarding.

Ye Bike Shop

There are all kinds, small to large, plain to exotic, and in every case, their job is to ensure you get the right bike, properly set up and adjusted and ready to ride, and to supply further advice and maintenance as necessary. You can also buy bikes from discount centres and by mail order, strictly on price. False economy, because bikes from these outlets are sold in a box and must be assembled and adjusted. This requires genuine expertise and a range of specialised tools.

Bike shops provide service, and the first marker for a good shop is that you feel comfortable there. Ideally, within two to three minutes of walking into a shop, you should be approached by a salesperson and straightaway politely asked if you are interested in a bike and, if so, what you have in

Opposite: Rare species (against wall) – an affordable used mountain bike

mind to do with it, and roughly how much you would like to spend. You should then be pointed toward two or three appropriate bikes. If, however, you are ignored, or glibly informed: 'Anyone who knows anything is riding a Wonder Star,' or otherwise given short shift or made to feel lame, then give courtesy and take your leave.

BALLANTINE'S GOLDEN RULES OF BIKE BUYING

Tai Chi masters often describe how to accomplish extraordinary things with disarmingly simple statements. What I have to tell you about buying bikes is simple but important.

» Look only at bikes that fit you. (See the chapter on Fit, p. 112) It does not matter what marvellous thing a bike is, if it does not fit you, it is no use.
» Prize light weight above all else. No matter what is said about features or bells and whistles, first thing, pick up a bike and see how light (or heavy!) it is. At even money between a new but heavy bike and a used but light bike with OK mechanics, I'd go for the used. Every time. Light weight first!
» Like the bike. Riding is about how well you get on with a bike, not the number of features it has, or a value-for-money price tag. Out of any given group of prospective bikes, 'best' is the one you like the most.

Assuming a proper welcome, when you discuss your needs and options, take care not to wring out underpaid bike shop staff. Some folks feel buying a £150 bike rates two hours of conversation about technical details. Sorry, no! A few questions are legitimate, but keep it to a few minutes, please!

Keep looking until you score a shop you like. Any decent-size town will have at least a few good shops. For help finding one, simply ask cyclists! At least some of the bikes in your neighbourhood will have come from nearby shops. Stop them in the road if you have to. A few polite queries of cyclists should point to the shops that might be good for you. A call to your local cycle campaign group will probably yield useful suggestions.

The more local a shop, the more convenient, but larger shops further away may have a wider selection. If you are looking for a specialised machine, such as a recumbent or cargo bike, then find a shop that deals in that particular type.

OK, you are in a shop you like, looking at two or three possible bikes. Early on, confirm that the shop provides a free post-sale bike maintenance check. This is mandatory, because as a new bike wears in, parts and bits loosen and require tightening. Hence the essential need, after 50 to 100 miles or so, for a mechanic to go over the bike and check that everything — repeat, everything — is properly adjusted and secure.

Buy a bike only after riding it. Do test rides when the choices are narrowed down to two or three machines you might actually purchase. Go for a proper ride of a couple of miles, under varied conditions. Keep in mind, a new bike may not be what you are used to, the brakes may be lively, the gears work in a different way, etc. Still . . . you should like it, and when you do — buy the bike!

Whoa . . . if you need accessories (see the chapter on Clobber p. 93), say, a rear carrier rack, a couple of locks, and a helmet, see if you can score a bike and bits package deal at a savings over what you would pay for the items if purchased separately. Do not press too hard.

Used

Here is a guide to depreciation from new price:

I year	80%
2 years	70%
3 years	60%
4 years	50%

These figures are guideline only, because condition, or mileage, is important. Reason is, manufacturers buy in components as original equipment (OEM) so cheaply, the cost of a new bike may less than buying the components separately. Hence, a really clapped-out bike has almost nil value.

Only £22! Single-speed and the saddle is no gift, but great value for money and charming, too.

A NICE STORY

Want a nice story? Here is one. Henny asked me to help her buy a bike. She had found a marvellous shop, Recycles, specialising in used bikes and end of year close-outs. The place was an Aladdin's Cave of bikes of all kinds, but we quickly homed in on a new Giant roadster that was just right: very light, good equipment, and a snip at Henny's top budget figure of £150, cash. Problem: too big.

There wasn't anything else suitable on the floor, so I began eyeballing the stock of mountain bikes, looking for a machine that I could modify with mudguards, a rack, and so on into a lightweight town bike. At the same time, I kept on at the proprietor: 'Hey, we really like the Giant. Is there any way you could get one in the right size?' After the third or fourth go, the proprietor sighed and said: 'Follow me'.

We trekked down through the shop, out the back, and up stairs and through hallways and what-else into a large room filled to bursting with more bikes, and out of a dusty corner rolled a spanking-new Ridgeback roadster in exactly the right size, just as lightweight as the Giant, and also £150, cash. A test ride, a couple of tweaks, and Henny was on her way.

We hit lucky. But also because we had a clear focus on what Henny wanted and could afford.

For a rule of thumb, any bike under £200 should be in good nick and not need replacement parts beyond minor bits such as cable wires or brake shoes. Major components (freewheel, chain set, gear changers) are expensive, as are shop rates for mechanical work. A bike that sold new for £200 now going used at £75 is no snip if it needs £100 worth of repairs!

A HEALTHY BIKE

» No paint wrinkles (or fresh paint) on forks and frame, especially on underside of top and down tubes, near the head tube. Paint wrinkles indicate possible frame damage from a crash.

» Sound cable housings and wires, without kinks or fraying.

» Clean, lubricated chain. To test for wear, lift a link on the chain ring. If it clears the tooth, the chain is well worn.

» Chain ring and freewheel sprockets: pointy or shark-shaped teeth indicate wear.

» Chainset should rotate smoothly, without side-to-side play. If rough or loose, bottom bracket may be shot.

» Pedals should spin smoothly, without lateral play.

» Brake pads should be evenly worn. If misshaped, or down to a nubbin, rims may have been damaged.

» Wheels should spin smoothly. Roughness may indicate damaged bearings. Test for side-to-side play by grasping top of wheel from side and pushing to and fro; a light click is OK, but lots of movement is not good.

» Check rims for impact damage (bulges) and wear. Spin wheels while holding a pencil or other object next to the rim. Side-to-side motion should not be over 5 mm.

» Spokes should be evenly tight on each side of the wheel.

» Forks should rotate freely, without roughness or binding. Test by holding handlebars, applying front brake firmly, and rocking bike to and fro (overleaf). A definite clicking from the head tube area is likely to be a loose head set.

» Test cranks for tightness: position cranks parallel to ground and press down on both pedals at once; then flip cranks 180° and press pedals again. If there is distinct 'click', a crank may be loose.

However, a quality bike that sold new for £500, and still in good condition except for damaged wheels, could be worth, say, £150, allowing £100 for a new set of wheels.

I have already given quite a few hints and tips about buying used bikes. Trying to explain all the things to look for when checking over a used bike would be inappropriate. I have to assume you are relatively unfamiliar with bike mechanics, and give the following general advice.

» Seek a clean machine in good condition, that passes the basic tests listed for A Healthy Bike, p. 88-89. Later on, when you know more about mechanics, you can try for extraordinary gems and bargains. For now, be happy to pay a fair price for a reasonable bike.

» Use your related skills. If you deal with or through friends and associates at work or school, establishing the history of a bike for sale is likely to be straightforward. It belongs to your brother-in-law's best friend, who purchased it last year — that sort of thing.

» If you have a bike-knowledgeable friend assist you, great, but take care to strain neither your friendship nor your friend's expertise. Your friend's job is to help; the buy is your decision and responsibility. Bikes at under, say, £150, are 'as is'. Above this amount, it may be worth buying 'subject to survey', meaning you and the seller agree a price, and you then pay to have the bike inspected by a bike shop. If everything is fine, you go ahead; if there is some problem, you re-negotiate or back out.

Opposite: Lock front brake, rock bike back and forth and listen for clicking

Clobber

Cyclists need clothes for weather protection, lamps for night-time riding, tools and kit for bike repairs, perhaps a couple of locks, and some organised means for dealing with all this clobber!

Clothing

On short-distance rides wear whatever you have on, subject to any provision for weather protection (see below). On longer rides, the three basic options are to wear: (1) cycling clothes; (2) regular clothes; and (3) cycling clothes and change to regular clothes at destination.

Clothes for cycling are trim and light, and designed with attention to key details such as not having lumpy seams in untoward places. They make riding a lot more efficient and fun, and are fine for general use, too. Of course many people prefer to wear regular clothes when not cycling and some — prison warders and students, for example — must don uniforms when working. Best is if you can keep a change of clothes where you need them. You can then wear cycling clothes and ride as hard as you want, and after doing the Superman-in-a-phone-booth bit and a clean-up, appear dapper or uniformed, as needs be.

Tips: cycle engines run hot and need to dissipate as heat four to five units of energy for every unit of energy put through the pedals. If it is cold outside, then it is normal and in fact good to be chilly at the start of a ride, and to become more comfortable after a mile or two after you warm up.

In warm weather it is commonplace to be comfortable and dry while riding (air-cooled engine), but break into a sweat on stopping. If you want to look spruce for a meeting with a bank manager or whatever, plan ahead and allow time for a cool-down period at journey end, and/or a visit to a washroom if one is available. A small washcloth takes up little space in a backpack, but (moistened with a shot from a water bottle) can provide a welcome fresh-up.

Weather: in bright summer you can whiz around in shirt and shorts and get away with it; the rest of the year, you need to be able to cope with variable conditions. This is best done by layering, e.g. using several items of clothing which can be added or removed as required, rather than relying on a single, bulky all-in-one garment.

Jacket

A jacket is your principal defence against wind, wet and cold. Most adaptable is a light shell in a breathable fabric that repels rain but allows at least some of your perspiration vapour to escape. Folded or rolled up, a shell takes up little space, and is easy to pack along for in-case use. I prefer zip-up (with flap), for flexible ventilation, but slip-over will do. Go for a loose fit, so other clothes can be worn underneath as required; the jacket can then be useful even in a howling blizzard.

A quality jacket will set you back a fair few quid. Keep in mind, you will use it lots, and want it to work. Avoid cheap plastic or vinyl throw-away jackets. They are hideous to wear, and frequently crack or tear. If economy is a must, an ordinary large bin-liner makes a surprisingly effective emergency rain jacket. (Tear holes for head and arms.) You can have a year's supply for a few quid. Best are extra-large, heavy-duty green garden waste liners.

As well as using an all-season, all-places jacket, I am also fond of lightweight, trimly-cut cycling jackets. British weather is often nippy, and there is something fine about riding wearing a jacket that is light and easy-moving and cosy so long as you keep moving. Most jackets of this type will shrug off a bit of rain, but not a steady downpour. If you have sorted sizes right, a cycling jacket can be topped with a shell, for a significant increase in warmth.

Shirts and More

Everyone has their own preferences. Mine is for natural cotton T-shirts and sweatshirts. Other folks like modern polyprop fabrics that help wick away perspiration, and dry quickly. Fleeces are effective. In winter, I especially like a vest, fleece or down-filled. It keeps the body core warm, but allows freedom of movement.

Pants

In summer, most cyclists wear shorts. In low temperatures, cycle pants are the route to go — again, trim-cut and cosy. Regular clothes work, too, but best if the bike has a chain guard to prevent stains. Cyclists who ride year-round generally like to have a pair of waterproof over-pants. In rainy but warm weather, I often wear just the over-pants, to avoid over-heating.

Gloves

I rarely ride without gloves. I want padding to protect shallow nerves in my palms, and protection in the event of a fall. In cold weather gloves are essential.

Shoes

Keen cyclists prefer clip-in pedals and shoes to match. The shoe has a built-in cleat that clips to the pedal when the rider pushes it into place, and releases by twisting the foot. (Such pedals are sometimes called 'clipless', a confusing term meant to distinguish the design from platform pedals fitted with toe clips and straps.) Clip-in pedals are great. The rider is firmly connected to the bike, yet can easily disengage from the pedals at any time. Clip-in is best for pedalling efficiency, bike control, and rider comfort.

Shoes for clip-in pedals are available in a variety of styles, from sandals to trainers to straight shoes to racing models. One type mounts the cleat on top (proud) of the sole, and is only used for racing, as walking is limited to an awkward duck-waddle. Another type recesses the cleat within the sole, to facilitate normal walking. However, this is OK only for short distances; few of these shoes are comfortable for extended walking.

People who have to be on their feet a lot will want proper shoes. As well, style is a consideration. So, for various reasons, one may prefer to wear regular shoes and cycle using conventional platform pedals. This is fine.

A compromise is a dual-model pedal: clip-in on one side, open on the other. Works for many people, but personally, I do not care for them. In traffic, it is important to be able to catch your pedal quickly and positively when starting off. With two-way pedals, whether you are wearing cleats or regular shoes, half the time you catch the 'wrong' side of the pedal and an insecure grip. You've got to back off and re-set your foot on the other side of the pedal. I find this a nuisance, and prefer to set up my bikes with either open or clip-in pedals, and wear the appropriate shoes.

Tip: if regular shoes are your preference but you would like a solid connection to the bike, consider old-fashioned 'rat-trap' pedals with toe clips and straps. Once you learn the knack of tapping a pedal so that it is in the right position to engage your foot, rat-traps are quick to use.

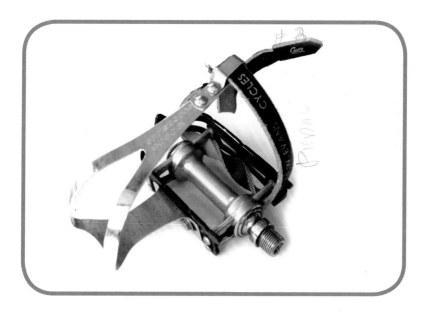

Rat-trap pedal (me old Campag)

Helmet

A helmet is useful if you fall off your bike. It is no help in a violent collision with a motor vehicle. And yet, insurance companies regularly try to reduce payments to cyclists who were not wearing a helmet when in collision with a motor vehicle. Just so you know, this is pure money-grubbing trickery, as every such case tried in court with the benefit of expert testimony has gone against the insurance company. Reason: a helmet gives a cyclist no advantage in a collision with a motor vehicle.

Indeed, one line of thought is that helmet-wearing generates a false sense of safety that leads to increased chance-taking and more frequent accidents. Therefore, if no one used helmets, the active practice of safety would improve, and accidents would be fewer.

Perhaps so. But you know, I took up wearing helmets well before they became popular, and the reason is still the same. Most cycle accidents are simple falls off the bike. Most severe and fatal accident injuries are to the head. If you fall or are thrown off your bike and bash your noggin, a helmet will materially reduce injury.

As for improving safety, cyclists have only one true mortal danger: motorists. For this, the best thing you can do is learn how to ride well. A helmet is something you use in case you should have a fall. And if you sometimes forget to wear a helmet, or just cannot be bothered, then relax and enjoy the wind in your hair.

Lights

Cities are well-lit: for what do you need lights? Lights are not for you to see by, but for you to be seen by others. City lights or no, at night cyclists without lights are often invisible. On behalf of motorists and pedestrians and other critters, I beg you to please use lights at night. It costs some money and bother, but is a consideration due to others that might well benefit you, too.

Dynamo lighting systems are the most economic. They are quite reliable and have good power for regular road riding. Problem is, they are permanently mounted on the bike, which is tenable only if you always ride point to point with utterly secure parking in both places. If you lock on the street, even just now and again, the lamps are vulnerable to vandalism.

First choice for street cycles are battery-powered LED lamps with quick-release mountings. Batteries last a long time, and lamps can be programmed to emit a steady light or blink in various eye-catching patterns. When not in use, the lamps are slipped into a pocket or backpack. Alas, a decent pair of LED lights will noticeably dent your wallet.

Conventional battery-powered lamps generally cast a stronger light, but are costly to operate. More economic are rechargeable systems, which can use one or more lamps at a range of power settings and beam patterns. There can be a low-watt flood for town use, and a high-intensity spot for dark country lanes. Dandy if you need to see where you are going, and hence popular for off-road night-time riding. Otherwise, seriously expensive, and absolutely not the sort of kit you can leave on a bike locked on the street.

Mechanical Survival

Your baseline mechanical kit should include a spare inner tube, a puncture repair kit with tyre levers, a small pump or air cartridge, and whatever tool or tools are needed to remove a wheel. Include a couple of zip ties and a bit of tape. We'll talk more about mechanical kit later, when going over basic maintenance and repairs.

Humping

How do you manage all this clobber? There are various answers, pick and choose.

If you have a rack, then a simple hold-all bag will do. Or a pannier. I prefer a sling bag, because it is easy to manage when off the bike. It holds gear with room to spare. When I use my working bike, I toss a sling bag or backpack into the broccoli crate, along with a couple of monster-size locks. For my sport machines, I generally use a small saddle pouch for tools and a spare inner tube. Typically, I carry only a lightweight in-case lock. For mountain bikes, I am fond of top-mounted handlebar bags. These will hold a few clothes or whatever, and a jacket or a big lock can be lashed on top.

Sling bags, bottom left, are handy and stay with you.

Saddle bags (above left) are a neat way to carry a spare tube, basic tools, and bits. A toe strap (bottom right) fastening is quick and tight. There are also models with quick-release clips, so you can easily remove the bag when locking on the street.

Bike Sizing And Set-up

Bike size, type of components, and set-up of saddle, handlebars, and pedals, are important to the efficiency and comfort of a bike for a rider. Sport bikes tend to follow pre-set forms, partly because designs are often dictated by sport governing authorities. City cycles are not subject to such restrictions, and make use of a wide range of design and equipment options.

Bike Size

In the past, bike size was measured by the distance between the bottom bracket and intersection of seat and top tubes.

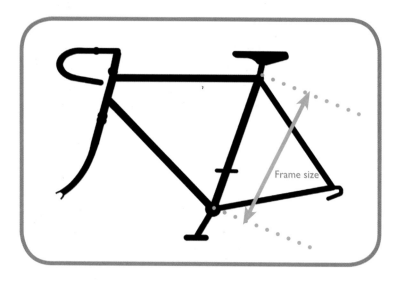

Frame size

That worked so long as top tubes were horizontal. These days, frames commonly feature sloping top tubes, or no top tube, and bike size is a relative concept. Aside from custom-built machines, bikes are produced in three sizes: small, medium, and large. Adjustments to fit individual physiques are made by varying the positions of the saddle and handlebars.

The right size of bike for you depends on your leg length, torso length, and riding style. Frames are usually proportioned; as height increases, so does length (distance between seat and head tubes). This works for people of average proportions. However, someone with long legs and a short torso on a bike sized for their legs may find themselves over-stretched between saddle and handlebars. Conversely, someone with short legs and a long torso and arms, again on a bike 'right' for their legs, could be tilted too far upright and have too much weight on the posterior.

First thing, sort out how you stack up. If you are long-legged relative to your torso, keep in mind that you may want a 'smaller' frame size, so as to not be over-stretched. If you are short-legged with a long torso, you may like a 'bigger' frame size, with enough room to stretch out.

Gender note: women tend to have longer legs/shorter torsos then men. Some manufacturers produce bikes specifically proportioned for women, and any good bike shop will be conversant with this topic. Nonetheless, most bikes are designed for men. Especially if you are a female looking at used bikes, beware of over-stretch!

Female-specific design

The shorter top tube and higher front end of the female-specific Condor Bellissima gives a better fit for women with long legs/short torsos.

Overstretched

Kathy is happy, but the borrowed bike (Henny's) is too long, and so her arms are stretched out and stiff. This will cause soreness and pain in the neck and back.

About Right

Life's ironies — Henny is on Kathy's bike, and looking good; her arms are slightly flexed, and able to help absorb bumps and road shock at the front wheel. Her back is slightly rounded, so her hips can more easily rise to help absorb bumps at the back wheel.

In Contrast

Kathy's back is dished inward. This stiffens the spine, and prevents the hips from flexing relative to the torso. Bumps and road shock are transmitted straight up to the brain. Not comfy.

Next, sort your general style. People who prefer a more upright, relaxed riding position are often advised to opt for a larger frame size. One reason: with contemporary headset designs, handlebars can only be raised by a small amount, if any. The other way, people who favour a dynamic, active riding style, are usually told to opt for a smaller frame size. Partly, this is so the rider can get down low, for better aerodynamics and quicker bike handling.

If you are going for a mountain bike and plan to do vigorous off-road riding, definitely go for a smaller (relative to your height) frame. You want the top tube well distant from your crotch — when straddling the frame, there should at least 4 inches of clearance between crotch and top tube.

My personal preference for a town bike is a smaller frame size. There is a little less bike (weight), handling is quicker, and pedal response is a shade more lively . . . but honestly, it is probably mostly a matter of style. Unless carting home a 20-kilo load of groceries, or a stack of timber for a building project, I tend to go as well as I can. My normal position is somewhat forward, with weight balanced between pedals, saddle, and handlebars. I'm well placed to float a bump, crack on a little juice, or quickly change direction.

By way of contrast, my son, who is fit and strong and also uses a bike as his main transport, has a supremely laid-back, relaxed riding style. At his request, I have modified his mountain bike until it more resembles an old Dutch roadster than a machine originally intended for sport. It works just fine for him.

As said, bike size is relative, and I hope you don't find this confusing. There simply is no agreed yardstick. Manufacturers vary in the methods they use to calculate frame size; a frame sized as 18-inch by one company, can be listed as 15-inch by another firm.

Still, general sizing is pretty straightforward. For height, you are either small, medium, or tall, and you look at either small, medium, or large bikes. Depending on manufacturer, some bikes will be borderline; in one range, medium may fit well, in another, medium may be on the large side. The point, really, is to be conscious of the issue, and take note of which bikes seem to suit you best.

Keep in mind, the 'size' of a bike and how it feels for fit is the sum of several variable elements that need to be considered in relation to each other. More on this after a discussion of gears and brakes.

UP OR DOWN?

With large frames, the tendency is for the top tube to slope down from the head tube; with small frames the tendency is to slope up from the seat tube. Six of one, half a dozen of the other? Nope. With smaller frames, often the head tube is longer (hence higher) than it would proportionally be on a larger frame. This is to give the rider a more upright riding position, which is useful in traffic, or for off-road trials. Conversely, a road time trial bike may well go for a shorter head tube, to help lower the rider into a deep, aerodynamic tuck.

Gears and Brakes

Gears

Choice of gearing system has a major effect on the character of a bike. For a chain-drive, there are two options: internal hub gears, or external derailleur gears.

Internal hub gears nest within a shell, protected from weather and dirt, and need no maintenance beyond regular lubrication. The chain is stout and strong and can be enclosed inside a chain guard or cover. This keeps out dirt and reduces maintenance and extends chain life. As well, clothing and skin are protected from oil stains, a feature which is really nice when you are well turned out and want to stay that way.

Shimano Alfine Hub Gear

On the operation side, hub gears can be shifted at any time to any gear, whether the bike is in motion or stationary. This is useful when there is a rapid change of pace, or if you stop quickly, without changing gear.

Traditional objections to hub gears are limited choice of gear ratios, and energy loss due to the mechanical inefficiency of indirect gears. Perhaps decades ago. Modern hub gears have plenty of ratios; 8- and 9-speed hubs are now widely available, and one high-tech model has 14.

As for efficiency, some of the latest multi-speed hubs appear to be pretty slick. In particular, Shimano's new Alfine 8-speed hub looks promising. I do not have hard test data, but the word from experienced designers is that the Alfine initially has some noise and resistance, but after a few hundred miles quiets down and smoothes out.

Derailleur gears are the first choice for sport. Provided the transmission is clean, they run with optimum efficiency. Shifting modern indexed systems is easy enough, but the cranks must be turning in order to change gear. On the maintenance side, derailleur gears are exposed to dirt and wet, and need regular servicing. External mounting renders them vulnerable to chance knocks and damage in the event of a fall.

In sum, hub gears need minimal maintenance, are easy to use, and are clean. Performance can be pretty good. Derailleur gears need more maintenance, and more skill to use, but give top performance.

The big point to take on board is that once, hub gears were only associated with heavy roadster bikes. These days, it is entirely feasible to have a true lightweight bike with hub gears, especially in models designed for urban use. Hub gears have a lot of advantages, especially for riders new to cycling, or who have not used derailleur gears.

Gear Shift Controls

Gear shift controls have two basic designs: twist-grip, or various arrangements of small levers and buttons. Twist-grip operates by rotating a ring mounted just inboard of the handlebar end grip. Last time I looked, this design had the fewest moving parts and was easy to service. Lever/button designs are configured to be operated while gripping the handlebar end, and are easy to use. Some models are mechanically rather complex. Both twist-grip and lever/button designs usually have display indicators to show which gear is in use. This can be a useful aid to maintaining good chain alignment between front chain rings and rear sprockets. Which is best is a matter of personal preference. This is something to sort for yourself on a few test rides.

Older bikes may have shift levers in all sorts of places: on the down tube, handlebar ends, and along the handlebars. Modern drop-handlebar bikes typically combine brake and shift controls in a single lever.

Twist grip   Lever / button

Trigger for 3-speed hub gear

Brakes

Broadly, there are three types of brakes: rim, hub, and disc. Rim brakes are the most common and work fine for most circumstances. They are lightweight, relatively inexpensive, and easy to maintain. For town use, V-brakes are the best, as they are powerful, and do not need strong lever pressure to operate.

Hub brakes are enclosed, and hence usually perform well even in wet conditions. They need little maintenance, and are durable. In years past, hub brakes were typically heavy, and fitted only to stout roadsters and tandem bikes. Modern units are increasingly lightweight — and as you might easily guess, are increasingly featured on lightweight town bikes.

Hub brake

V-brake

Disc brake

Dual action calliper brake

Disc brakes are the business — very powerful, with lots of depth, which means control is good even at extreme braking forces. Just the ticket if you are hurtling a mountain bike down a steep trail, or screaming along at 45 MPH plus in an HPV. Strictly speaking, they have more performance than is necessary for most high streets. They are costly, and maintenance can be exacting.

Most brake levers can be adjusted to suit individual hand size or grip. The idea is to be able to ride with two fingers around the handlebar, and two fingers on the brake lever, poised for instant action. Two things, then: the lever has to be set so that it is within reach of the braking fingers, and the brake has to engage while the lever is still clear of the gripping fingers. Setting the lever is easy; there will be a small screw on the brake lever mount, usually just inboard of the cable and barrel adjuster. Setting the point where the brake engages is done with the barrel adjuster, and if necessary, the cable anchor bolt. See the Maintenance chapter for details.

HEED — Modern bike brakes are very effective. To develop safe braking technique, please be sure to do the braking drills in the Bike Handling Skills chapter.

Gears and Brakes — Summary

Times are changing. Roadsters and town bikes used to be heavy and low-tech, only lightweight sport machines featured exotic components. Today, roadsters and town bikes can be true lightweights, specified with the latest equipment. As an indication of how things are going, the new Shimano Alfine 8-speed hub gear has a fitting for a disc brake. In the pipeline (from another manufacturer) is a 9-speed hub gear with a carbon fibre shell.

The Set-Up

How a bike fits you is easily as precise as the fit of a shoe. In this department, details and fine increments matter. Hence, I take you through the whole program, and some of the information is quite technical. Use it in a general way when first setting up a bike, and then go for refinements after you have done some miles and have a feel for what suits you best.

By me, bikes should be sold sans saddle, pedals, stem, and handlebar. Reason: these items are crucial to the fit and comfort of a bike, and what is good for Ed may not suit Paul. If you are buying a new bike, consider your personal fitting needs, and negotiate exchanges before settling on a final price. Purchased separately, a nice saddle, good set of pedals, and a decent stem, can easily whiz most of £100. On an exchange basis the sting should be less.

One short-cut: many bike shops have fitting machines. These are static 'bikes' that are adjustable in every dimension. You climb aboard and pedal, and the technician then moves things around to realise the best configuration for the position which is optimal for you. Advantage: no waste of money replacing components for a different fit. Also, if there are physical problems, such as one leg shorter than the other, or a tendency for the foot to twist while pedalling, these can be identified and dealt with when setting up the bike.

This kind of service is not available in grocery stores!

Sizing frame

Saddle Position

Height

When seated on the saddle, with your heel on the pedal and as far away from you as possible, your leg should be straight but not stretched. Much more height, and you risk rocking your hips as you pedal. Lower, and pedalling is harder work and more stressful on the knees. If you err in any direction, go to the high side. Various studies suggest that for *some* riders, a slight increase in height over 'normal' can increase power.

Fore-and-Aft

The fore-and-aft position of the saddle relative to the bottom bracket has an effect on height. Indeed, a common trick when climbing is to shift back in the saddle, for a little more power when thrusting. The greater importance of fore and aft location, however, is in the distance between the nose of the saddle and the handlebars. As you might expect, a longer distance will make a rider incline further forward to reach the bars. A crude measure is to place your elbow on the nose of the saddle and extend the arm toward the bars. On a time trial bike, the fingertips might be 6-7 cm from the bars; on road racing bike, 3-4 cm, and on a town bike, just brushing the handlebars.

Good leg extension

Saddle too low, reduces power, increases stress on knees.

Naturally, if the handlebars are on a stem that holds the bars very far forward, then using the elbow/fingertip measurement to set saddle fore-and-aft position could wind up with the saddle too far forward.

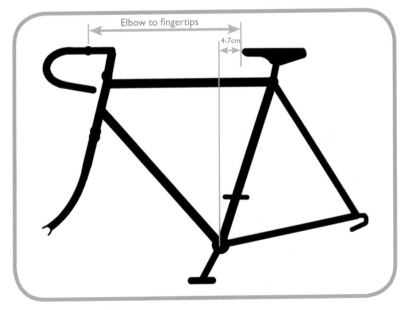

Saddle position

A classic means for determining 'correct' fore-and-aft saddle position is to set the height about right, then seat the rider with one pedal in the forward position (3 or 9 o'clock). A plumb (vertical) line from the knee should bisect the pedal axle. Sounds scientific and techie, but I've never been able to find any justification for this oft-quoted guideline. Moreover, on recumbent cycles the knee-pedal relation tends to the horizontal rather than vertical.

Optimum fore-and-aft saddle position for an upright bike depends mostly on riding style. For example, saddles on time trial bikes tend to be well forward. A time trial, or 'race of truth', is against the clock, and riders ride as fast as they are able over a set distance. Note, however, that TT riders tend to have low-set bars and to adopt a fierce 'tuck' for aerodynamic efficiency. In such a configuration, moving a little forward may help open the lungs and facilitate easier breathing.

RECUMBENT CYCLES

With recumbent cycles the seat to bottom bracket distance is set roughly the same way as with an upright bike: when comfortably seated, with the heel of the foot on the pedal, and the pedal as far from the rider as possible, the leg should be almost fully extended.

I myself prefer a somewhat forward saddle position, for the simple reason that I find it more comfortable. I do not like carrying much weight on my hands, and shifting forward puts a little more weight on my feet. In contrast, the usual norm for long-distance tourists is to have the saddle in a slightly rearward position.

Which means — you should experiment for yourself. Your body is not going to shrink or expand to fit to the bike! Especially when starting out with a bike, take the time and energy to move the saddle around and see how it works and feels at different settings. It's a bit of work, but well worthwhile if you find a sweet perch.

Tilt

Set the saddle dead level. Use a spirit level if need be. Or balance a long board or broomstick on the saddle and ensure it does not incline up or down. If you want to tilt, make very small changes. The danger with raising the nose is possible harm to your reproductive gear. The other way, tilting the nose down risks pushing you forward, increasing strain on the hands and wrists as you exert force to stay in position. As well, bumps may tend to pitch you forward, reducing control at the exact moment when you need it. If you have a plush, comfy saddle, allow for compression.

Cranks

Crank length has a big effect on pedalling efficiency and comfort. Yes, cranks come in different lengths, and one mark of cheap bikes is the use of cranks of the same length, regardless of frame size.

This short-changes folks with short legs, because to rotate the cranks, short legs have to bend more than long legs, increasing wear and tear on the knees. Please believe, you want to keep stress on the knees to a minimum. In a nutshell, this is done by learning to pedal properly, spinning the cranks lightly and rapidly, and by using cranks of a length appropriate for your general height and/or leg length.

As to what is appropriate, the current trend is toward shorter cranks. Convention says for people 1.8 m tall or higher, 175 mm cranks; for people 1.65 m to 1.8 m tall, 170 mm cranks; and for people 1.65 m or less, 165 mm cranks. You can chop another 5 mm easy. I normally ride 170 mm but have been using 165 mm without a ripple. Soon enough, I'm going to try 155 or even 150 mm.

I do not want to get too technical, but after all, what you do with a bike is pedal it, so this topic matters. In particular, there are lots and lots of mountain bikes out there with 175 mm cranks, regardless of frame size. Roadsters, too, tend to be uniform, this time at 170 mm. That's OK for people of average height or taller, but what about everyone else?

If you are on a super-economy budget, rooting an abandoned bike out of someone's shed, then changing crank size is not an affordable option. But if you are laying down a few hundred quid for a new bike, then ensure that the cranks are the right length for you.

Pedals

Fit a pedal? Yes indeed! There are two main things to consider: the type of pedal you would like to use, and whether any special adjustments are needed for your physique. Again — almost a mantra — some of this information is rather technical; use it as required.

Pedals [clockwise from left]

Wide BMX platform pedals with studs; classic quill pedals with toe clips and straps; dual platform/step-in pedals; single side step-in pedals, for racing.

Open pedals can be used with any kind of shoe. Disadvantages: it is hard to maintain a fast cadence (revolutions per minute of the cranks), and in adverse circumstances such as hitting a bump or pot-hole, there is risk of losing a pedal.

If you are new to bikes you might imagine that in a difficult moment, you would want to be able to stick your foot out. Take it from me, you do not! The pedals are a primary means for controlling a bike, and trouble can be defined as not having a firm connection to the pedals. Imagine hitting a series of bumps with your legs splayed to either side.

Sport riders used to use cage pedals with toe clips and straps, paired with slotted cleats mounted on a shoe. The slot fitted over the rear cage, and when the strap was snugged down, the rider was firmly attached to the pedal. Indeed, a classic sequence (me, too) was for a rider to forget the straps, stop, and then slowly topple over. Another problem with this system is that the foot is locked into one plane of rotation. As it happens, the way legs and knees work for many folks, pedalling causes the foot to twist from side to side. If natural twist is inhibited, damage to the knee can result.

The happy ending of this story is the clip-in pedal. With this design, there is no toe clip and strap. The cleat is recessed into the sole of the shoe, so that it is possible to walk normally when off the bike. (All-out racing models use raised cleats, for a larger area and better foot support.) To engage the cleat the rider inserts the cleat in position, and presses to clip in. To disengage, the foot is rotated a few degrees. With some models, the foot can also be disengaged by pulling up. Release tension is variable from very slight to rather hard.

Clip-in pedals have built-in 'float'; the foot can twist to either side for a few degrees before disengaging. This is important, because it reduces stress on the knees. Another advantage is no toe strap; set tight, these can numb the foot or chafe.

Shoes for use with clip-in pedals range from open sandals to winter boots. There are shoes for racing, touring, mountain biking, and calling by the bank. Some models are designed for walking and work pretty good. Still, there are times in life when you want proper shoes, either for style or function.

Dual Pedals

One option are dual pedals. One side is open, the other is clip-in. Sounds sensible, and is popular, especially with town riders. Another option is a clip-in pedal with a large platform. These can be used with regular shoes.

Open Platform

A proper platform pedal has a large surface area and will provide support for soft-soled as well as ordinary shoes. Traditional rubber platform pedals are a bit hazardous, because they can be slippery. BMX-style platform pedals studded with pins or adjustable screws provide a better grip.

Cage with Toe-clip and Strap

A cage or rat-trap pedal is designed to be used with cleats. However, they can be used with regular shoes, and on this count alone, are preferred by some cyclists. When used with toe clips and straps they are not as quick to release as clip-in pedals, but are safe enough so long as the straps are not over-tight. The big advantage over open pedals is being able to spin properly, and having a solid connection with the bike.

Stem

The stem holds the handlebars, and according to model and size, can have various degrees of rise (height) and reach (forward position). There are two types, quill and threadless. A quill stem inserts inside the steerer tube and is held with a bolt and wedge. A threadless stem fits over the top of the steerer tube and is held in place with clamps.

Clockwise from left: Threadless, Quill, and Quill showing wedge mechanism

Height

Height depends a lot on the kind of stem. A quill stem can rise as high as length will allow. The limit will be marked on the side of stem. To adjust, undo the stem bolt 2 or 3 turns and tap it with a rubber-coated tool or hammer and block of wood, to knock the wedge loose. Set the stem at the height you want. If you have grease handy, take the stem out and anoint the part that will be inside the steerer tube. This prevents corrosion and should be done at least once a year. Replace stem and tighten so it is firmly in place, but you can move the handlebars relative to the front wheel (hold it between your legs) without straining. This way, if you take a fall, the handlebars/front wheel will give without something bending or breaking.

A threadless stem can be raised only with the use of washers. Probably, the star nut inside will have to be moved, which requires a special tool. This is a job for a bike shop.

HOWEVER, for all stems, the amount of rise is also determined by the angle formed with the head tube, and the forward reach of the stem.

Reach

Reach is the distance forward from the elbow of the stem to the clamp that holds the handlebars. On a conventional road-racing bike, the upper portion of the stem is usually level, and hence easily sized. Stems of this type are described as 6 mm, 8 mm, 10 mm, and on, and usually, small bikes have short stems and big bikes have long stems. It's easy to deduce that if you have short legs and long arms, you may want a longer stem than usual.

Stems for flat bars are another ball game; rise may range from none to lots, and reach, too, may be small or considerable. It is down to what sort of design is used, and the only way to sort this between different bikes and stems is try and see. This is when it is handy to have a realistic idea of where you want the handlebars to be in relation to the saddle. Feel boxed? Read on . . .

Adjustable Stems

Yay! Salvation — adjustable stems. These are sometimes featured on roadster and town bikes and are a great idea. The elbow joint is adjustable, so both the rise and reach of the bars can be varied to suit different riding styles and riders. Adjustable stems tend to weigh a little more, but of course are versatile. Available in both quill and threadless models.

Above: Adjustable quill stem

This one is set for maximum height.

Below: Adjustable threadless stem

> ## ARM SPRINGS
>
> One way to check the saddle/stem/handlebar relationship is through the arms. When you ride, the arms should be slightly flexed, so they act as shock absorbers, bending and extending as the bike goes over bumps. If the reach is too far, the arms will tend to lock at the elbow. This makes for a jarring ride, and causes back strain. The other way, too short a reach also diminishes shock absorption through the arms, and by tilting the rider upright, places too much weight on the stern, which can become sore. As well, shocks are transmitted straight up the spine, which can cause headache.

Handlebars

Handlebars vary enormously in design and configuration. Herewith some general information and pointers.

Handlebars should be roughly shoulder width, to help keep the chest and lungs open for breathing. Wider gives more leverage and can be useful for off-road bikes. Narrower helps slim the rider profile and, naturally, may be used on fast bikes.

The four general configurations are bucket handle; flat; drop; and profile.

Bucket handle is the classic roadster type and suits an upright riding position. Flat is rarely strictly flat. Usually, the shape resembles a bird's wing, and hence the position of the bars and location of the grips depends on how the handlebar is clamped in the stem. To adjust, loosen the binder bolt or clamp on the stem.

Drop handlebars are typically used for road racing and touring bikes, and are made in various patterns. The hooks (sharply curved parts) allow a rider to tuck deep, for maximum aerodynamic advantage. This is rarely important for routine urban riding. However, riding on the hoods (brake lever/gear shift mounts) is fairly comfortable. For a rule of thumb, racers tend to set the lower portion of the hooks level with the ground. Town and touring riders often rotate the bars slightly upward, so that the ends point toward the ground at an angle of about 10°. This somewhat raises the rider position.

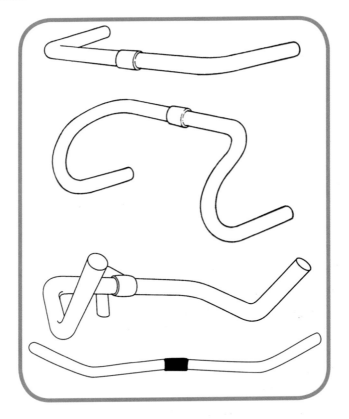

From top: Bucket - Drop - Profile - Flat

Profile bars are minimalist and, I have to say, quite comfortable. This configuration is normally associated with time trial bikes, but I like it for general use as well.

Flat bars can be modified to a profile shape with the addition of bar ends. These increase the number of riding positions and, depending on how the bar ends are angled, make it possible for the rider to assume a deeper tuck when pushing into a headwind. However, the fingers are no longer right on the brake levers.

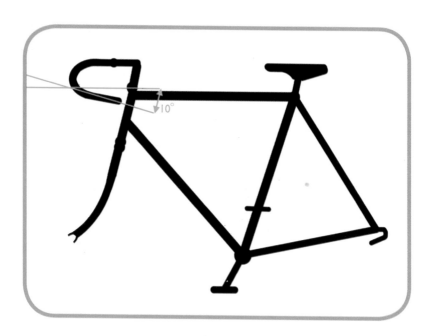

SAFETY HINTS

I'm turning right

DANGER

Give your signals promptly and clearly. Give the man behind a chance to act.

DANGER

Ride with caution, drive with care, be tolerant with other road users and make the roads safe for all.

Every cyclist should be familiar with the Highway Code, which can be obtained from any good stationer, price one penny.

Never rely on the "other man" to do the right thing—he may not.

Always signal your intention to turn, but make sure it is *safe* to do so.

Watch the movements of other traffic and when in doubt *stop*.

Never try to make pedestrians or cyclists "wake up" by ringing your bell close to them. It is likely to fluster them and make them jump or swerve in front of you.

Always proceed carefully over cross-roads, even though you are on the major road.

Tramlines, manhole covers and similar things call for additional care. Never attempt to

"Carry on George, I'm dropping behind; it's wrong to ride three abreast with all this traffic about."

SLOW
MAJOR ROAD AHEAD

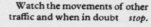

RIGHT HAND TURN

Make sure the road ahead is clear before pulling out; there may be a vehicle approaching on its wrong side.

take a narrow angle with tramlines. Man-hole covers sometimes protrude dangerously and, if it is necessary to ride over them, ride carefully and avoid the edges.

In wet weather particularly, never jam on your brakes, especially the front one. A gentle and firm pressure on the rear brake, helped where necessary by the front brake, is desirable. Remember rear wheel skids can often be corrected but

"I'll drop behind, Bill; where there's a bend there's always a risk. It's foolish to take chances."

SCHOOL

You can't be too careful with children around.
For their safety and

III:TACTICS

Route-finding

If you have not done much cycling or walking around your neighbourhood, then prepare for an education! It is usual to discover that places are located differently than you imagine, and — classic — that streets believed to be flat have definite gradients.

The first step is to obtain a decent map and give it a thorough study. Compact address-finder books are not so good, because they are too small to provide an overall picture. You want fairly big maps that cover a good stretch of territory with a fine level of detail. Londoners are blessed, because Transport for London (TfL) publishes a series of cycling maps which are so super, everyone, cyclist or not, wants them. They are free, and TfL has literally given away millions and millions.

Free or purchased, sit down with your map and look at some of the places you want to reach. Your needs may be simple, only a jaunt around the corner to pick up some groceries. More likely, you will want to journey a distance, to go to work, visit a sweetheart, or whatever.

First, use a ruler to lay out a straight line between your home (or other start point) and your destination. See 'how the crow flies' compares with the routes you already know and might use. There are apt to be some surprises, for example, a road you believed went straight to a place may actually go a long way around.

Next, check out possible routes. For purposes of analysis, think of routes as three main types:

» Primary – Arterial and main roads that carry large volumes of fast-moving traffic.

» Secondary – Back streets and cycle paths with low or medium volumes of vehicle traffic.

» Off-road – Canal tow paths, tracks, parks, etc.

See if you can lay out routes of each type. Obviously, possibilities will depend on circumstances. Your neighbourhood might be scant on off-road sections, for example. Do the best you can, bearing in mind that what you work out on paper is only a starting point for on-the-ground research.

The contour of the land is an important factor. A longer route that is fairly even may be a lot easier than a shorter route with several sharp climbs. An Ordnance Survey map with contour lines can be useful for planning, but again, the practical guide will be what you learn through simple trial and error.

Another important element is cross-traffic and junctions. For both speed and energy efficiency, you want a smooth ride. A longer route with few stops may be both quicker and easier than a shorter route with lots of stops and starts.

The best route for you will depend on your level of riding ability, your temperament and mood, and how things are going on the day. It is a bit of a chicken-and-egg problem, and one reason for knowing about different types of routes is so you can custom-tailor journeys according to circumstances. If you are feeling dreamy, you may want to meander along a riverside path. If you are late for work or feeling peppy, you may want to speed along a main route.

OK, out and rolling, and for a first journey, allow at least twice or even thrice the time you think you might need. You want to be able to stop often, and to take opportunities to explore. There are all sorts of things you will not know until you try or see them. For example, a route might include a roundabout that is genuinely hairy and difficult for cyclists. Is there another way? What about the next street over? Or cutting through a park?

The old-time mountain men who explored and pioneered North America generally always knew where they were. As a cyclist, this is your game, too. You are a physical being in a physical environment. Keep notes, if that is helpful, and certainly, refer back to your map. Look! That alley — might it link to the next high street? Eventually, you will know a great deal about where things are, and part of the fun of riding will be playing with both geography and topography.

Short-cut out of a dead-end street. If there are pedestrians, dismount and walk.

Of course, on your first few rides, it may not feel quite so wonderful. You may be hot, or cold, you may be upset with motorists, or feeling weak in the legs, or frightened you are in a bad neighbourhood, or whatever. Hey, this is normal. You have got to post a learning curve for knowing the best routes for you, and as well, for developing your riding technique and general savvy. Main thing: give yourself plenty of time. Be able to relax. If things get too whiskery and rough, get off your bike and walk for a while. The whole deal is that you work within your comfort range. Eventually, you'll learn the things you need to know, a good way around a monster hill, for example, or conversely, where to make one short, sharp climb, so that you can then flow with ease for a couple of miles along a gently sloping ridge.

You are aiming, curiously, to indeed become rather as one of the old-time mountain pioneers. They looked after themselves, and they knew where they were by the wind, the moss on the trees, the stars, and all the elements of the outdoors. You, too, are self-sufficient, and move with the land and terrain and all the things within it. It is a huge amount of fun, and especially if you follow a principle voiced by Bruce Lee for studying martial arts: not to rush, but to expand and stretch slowly, bit by bit. The core of cycling is that you are in control and set your own pace. That includes choosing where you go. Freedom.

Mixed-mode: Trains

Mixed-mode transport — using a train or bus for part of your journey — can be an efficient way of dealing with long journeys. Of course, there has to be an available service. In the UK, there are few if any buses with racks for bikes. Train services are inconsistent. Some carriers allow bikes, others do not. Those that do may impose restrictions at peak commuting times. Truth to tell, coping with a bike or pram on a crowded commuter train is difficult and stressful.

Working out a viable sequence for mixed-mode transport using trains starts with finding out which services permit bikes. If you live in a town like London, it is worth obtaining a good map of all train services, because many overlap and share stations. Route A might be out, but route B could be fine.

Do a trial run at an off-peak time. You need to check out details, such as which side of the train is best, and how to position your bike to minimise inconvenience to other passengers. You'll probably have to stand, so you can hold the bike and/or move it if necessary. Tip: have a bungee cord in your pocket; it can help secure the bike, or be used to hold down a brake lever for a parking brake.

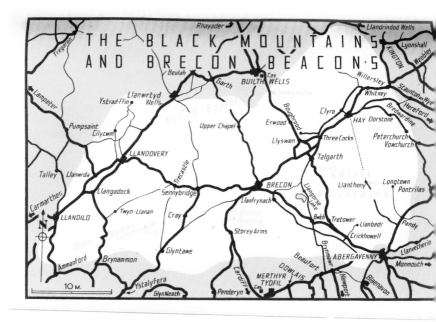

Nothing to do with urban living – this is prime mountain bike country!

Parking & Security

— The Right Way to Hang Bike Thieves —

Security is an ongoing concern for cyclists. Bikes are vulnerable to theft and vandalism. In public places, a strong lock will help deter theft but is not absolute protection. Locks can be broken or opened — not every time, nor by everyone — but often enough. More significantly, even if Merlin's ghost were to appear on a magic bicycle and bestow you with a lock as immutable as King Arthur's legendary sword-in-the-stone Excalibur, your bike still would not be safe. When thieves encounter locks that are not easily broken, they will often cut apart the bike frame to steal the components.

Bike security is a game in which you aim to stay a couple of jumps ahead of the thieves, and on your side, parking resources are the important factor. Good bikes have to be kept in safe places, such as inside homes and places of work. For locking up on the street and in public places (such as a school yard or railway station), the two strategies are either to have a low-value bike not worth stealing, or to use several locks, so that thieves seek easier pickings.

The case for a junk (or hack) bike is simple. The essence of a quality bike is light weight. Locking securely on the street requires using at least two strong locks of different types. The locks cost over £100 and are bulky and heavy; carrying them turns a lightweight bike into a heavyweight. A junk bike costs less and at less overall weight is physically easier, too. Figure £8 for a simple lock and £25 – £40 for a bike that works well enough for short trips. All-up weight is under 15 kg, or about half the mass of a lightweight bike laden with 2 heavy-duty locks. Less work to pedal, and less stress when locking on the street, because you don't fret about what might be happening to your machine. When a junk bike is nicked, there is irritation, but no big upset. You get another.

Ideally, you should have a quality bike as well. On rides, you can carry a lightweight in-case lock but otherwise, the machine stays with you. At a cafe, you sit outside, with one hand near the bike. Visit a friend, the bike rolls inside with you. Stop for a wizz, it's one hand for the bike and the other for conducting your business.

Is there a more elegant solution? Sure — hang bike thieves! Not dead. That would be too quick and kind. They should suffer. Better would be to lock them into public stocks outdoors for three to five days, in open weather. No food, no breaks. For a little water to maintain life, and in the interest of public hygiene and people downwind, they should be hosed off once a day.

I hate bike thieves. I do not accept any of the excuses or rationalisations for what they do. I cannot count how many worthwhile people I have known who have worked long and hard to earn the price of a fine, much-wanted new bicycle — and then Rip! had it stolen.

But there you go: bike theft is a pestilence. You have to ride with the flow.

It is interesting to note that in countries where cycling is popular, such as the Netherlands, there is a clear-cut division between basic utility and quality sport bikes. Sport cycles are kept inside at home, and go out on Sundays or early or late rides, and the locks used, if any, are strictly lightweight. Utility cycles spend a lot of time outside and typically have a built-in lightweight lock, to use when shopping, etc. A second, more robust lock is used when fastening down for the night or in high-risk areas. A point of interest: in cities such as Amsterdam, these bikes are regularly stolen by junkies. No one seems to get upset. One simply whisks around to the thieves' market and buys a similar bike, perhaps even the very one that was stolen, for about £20. It is almost a form of socialism.

One can have a good bike for fun, and a beat-up wreck for local use, but what if you have a long 10- or 15-mile commute and want to use a good bike? Answer: you set up secure parking at both ends of the journey, use a good bike, and carry a lightweight lock in case you need to stop to help out a fallen granny.

One reason for studying up on why cycling is so swell for everybody and everything is so you have ammunition when organising parking. For example, any employer will benefit from providing bike parking and should actively help employees to purchase bikes. If the place of work does not have a scrap of space to spare, then look around. What about other nearby businesses? Is there a laundry or restaurant or whatever, that might let you keep a bike in some out-of-the-way spot? How about a specialist cycle parking facility? These have secure bike parking, lockers, showers, and some will do repairs and servicing while you are off earning your crust.

If there is no inside parking, how about the fortress approach? You find a spot suitable for locking up — a stout pole or fence, in public view — and thereto keep a battery of locks, chains, and cables. Thieves usually pass on a bike festooned with locks. If vandalism is a problem, how about a folding bike? Not even that? Well, how about a change of job? I mean, you spend a lot of your life moving yourself around, and the time should be well used. Another job might not have the same money or status, but if it allows you to ride a bike, you will come out ahead.

Parking At School

To encourage cycling to school, the government has allocated funds for schools to spend on improving cycling facilities. The amount per school is up to £10,000, more than enough for providing cycle parking. The boodle is there free for the asking, and if you are a student and your school has done nothing about cycle parking, then your Good Civic Deed is ready on a plate!

Ensure that the best possible parking is created. The site must be near the main entrance, preferably within the school grounds, in full open view. It must not be round the back, or other obscure location, as this will promote theft and vandalism. The stand for locking the bike must be easy to get at, support the bike, and allow for locking the frame and both wheels. A simple stand in the open air is better than nought, but the ideal is a proper cycle shelter with a roof.

Get it to happen. If the school is unresponsive, persevere. For help, and a ton of information, contact Sustrans (0845 1130065 – www.sustrans.org.uk) and the CTC (0870 873 0060 – www.ctc.org.uk) and the DfT (020 7944 2978 – www.dft.gov.uk).

Parking At Home

Residential accommodation rarely includes provision for bike parking. You have to improvise. First and most common resort is to park a bike in a building entrance hall. Fine if there is enough room. If space is tight, a bike can be modified to fit tidily against a wall. The bolt that holds the handlebars is replaced with a quick-release lever and cam. Flick, and the bars can be spun to line up with the bike. The pedals are changed to quick-release, too, with a mechanism similar to that for garden hose fittings. Click click and the pedals are off. It all takes only seconds.

2D with pedals removed and bars turned

If several people live in a flat or house, and a number of them have bikes, then even with clever stacking there won't be room enough for all in the hall. Mind, too, that exit paths should be unobstructed in case of fire.

Look up, look down, look around. There may a niche under the stairs, space above because of a high ceiling, or even a closet. There are all sorts of clever gadgets available for storing bikes in odd places and positions. They can be stood on end, hung on racks, and even suspended in mid-air using ropes and pulleys. If all else fails, you can stick it in the bath tub or shower.

Got an outside shed? This can be convenient for keeping bikes out of the house, but always secure machines just as strongly as when locking on the street. Many thefts are from gardens and sheds.

I always like to have the working bike right by the door, ready to roll. For maximum security, it should be locked. This also ensures you will have a lock — and key — when you go out.

Locking On the Street

Use bikes a lot, and you will have to lock on the street. Here is the drill.

» Always lock. You might be inside a store for just a few seconds, but that is all the time a thief needs. For stop-and-go errands I carry a lightweight lock around my neck, handy to use when I stop for a newspaper or some shopping. Another tactic is to disable the bike by removing one of the wheels and taking it with you.

» Always lock in a public place, where people are around. Obviously, avoid a dark alley where a thief can work unseen. But even on an open street, pick and choose your location. A spot that is slightly out of the way may be significantly more vulnerable than one bang in the middle of everything. However, take care not to obstruct pedestrians.

» Use at least two different types of strong locks, three is better. You want thieves to look for easier pickings, i.e. bikes secured with only one lock.

Fancy saddles should be locked.

Position lock so key mechanism is not exposed or is at least harder to get at.

Also, there are various special tools for opening or breaking locks, but a thief is usually limited to one tool for a particular type of lock. Using two locks of different types will fox them.

» Run each lock through the frame and a wheel and around a solid, strong, immutable object. A proper Sheffield-type cycle stand is the most convenient for securing wheels and frame together. Do not use cycle racks where only the wheel is secured.

» Arrange locks so they are snug, with no room to insert a pry bar. Try to position lock mechanisms and other vulnerable bits on the inside, where they cannot be easily got at for a forcible attack.

» Remove accessories such as lights and computers, and the saddle/seat post, if it has a quick-release bolt.

» Always, always have spare keys, stashed in a safe place.

Street Bikes

Quick-release wheels are handy when mending punctures or taking down a bike in order to fit it into a small space, but are an invitation to theft. A partial solution is to replace the quick-release mechanism with hex-key bolts. However, when locking up you should still secure the wheels. For one thing, a thief might have a hex key, too. More importantly, a wheel is not all that easy to cut through. A hacksaw can slice right through a bike frame, but will struggle with a flexible tyre.

Lights must be the quick-release type that you can stick in your pocket. Bolt-on lights are no good; vandals just tear them off. The seat post needs to be secured with a bolt, not a quick-release, and ideally, the saddle should be locked to the bike.

Some folks camouflage their bikes by painting them with rough-finish paint and/or wrapping the frames with old inner tubes. This is also helps protect against scrapes from poles, railings, etc. My personal preference for frame protection is foam pipe lagging, as it is lightweight and easy to mount and remove. Of course, disguise may not thwart a thief who is knowledgeable about bikes.

PERFORMANCE-WARRANTED LOCKS

High security locks which promise a money pay-out if they fail on the job can cost £100 and more — are they any good? Yes and no! Bike lock technology is evolutionary: manufacturers design locks as good as they can for the money, thieves trial-and-error learn ways to defeat the locks, and makers then upgrade their designs (and prices). The strength of a lock depends on the state of play at the moment, and the game can move quickly. Not long ago, it was discovered that a top-line bike lock with a certain type of key mechanism could be opened with a biro. Even by children. To credit, the manufacturer eventually did the right thing and issued a recall and free upgrade. Still, locks with this particular type of key mechanism were produced for many years, and number in the hundreds of thousands. Many owners know nothing of the recall, and continue to use locks trusted to be strong and safe, when in fact they are open invitations to theft.

Are all high-security locks junk? Of course not. Some are good, or at least, good sometimes. The problem is predictability. This is when I see again the unhappy faces of friends who just had nice bikes stolen, and hear them saying "And I had a new lock!"

Heed: if you know where to shop, it is possible to purchase, legitimately and with no questions asked, tools which are master keys for lock mechanisms. Rely solely on a lock to protect a bike, and sooner or later you will take a hit. To have good bike security you must be proactive. As said, it is a game, and you have to play it better than the thieves.

Shopping And Haulage

The options for carrying things with cycles range from adding various kinds of accessories, to using cycles that are purpose-designed for haulage.

The first option is to use a shoulder bag or rucksack. This keeps the bike clean and lean, and is the preferred method for all sport machines. It is also favoured by commuters and others who frequently go on and off the bike. Your stuff simply moves with you, instead of having to be unloaded every time you stop. A clean, uncluttered bike is easier to handle when going up and down stairs and using trains.

A shoulder bag is fine for holding a few items, and a surprising amount of groceries can be stuffed into a rucksack, depending on the size. Importante: for cycling, a compact rucksack that moulds smoothly to your body is best. You cannot ride comfortably wearing a massive 100-litre pack designed for trekking, and if you cram the thing chock-full of groceries, you will likely topple over!

Using a shoulder bag or rucksack means moving lightly, and suits frequent forays for a few items. When you need a lot of stuff at once, or things that are heavy, you can use a cargo bike, if you have one, or a taxicab or delivery services.

Option two is to fit a bike with baskets and/or racks. Baskets are wonderful. They are so handy, because you can just sling whatever into them, and away you go. Traditional wicker baskets are stylish. More utilitarian are wire metal baskets with a quick-release mounting. These can be used as a basket while shopping, and left off the bike when not needed. There are both front and rear models. Baskets have the same limitation as rucksacks; heavy loads will compromise bike handling.

Racks are an involved topic. Proper touring racks are stoutly constructed in order to hold panniers firmly and allow a good amount of baggage to be carried without upsetting the stability of the bike. However, distributing weight evenly and safely requires having racks front and back, and two sets of panniers. Expensive. More importantly, contending with four panniers is real nuisance. Packing and unpacking involves coping with an endless number of buckles and drawstrings. If you lock the bike on the street, you've got to remove the panniers and shlep them about, wherever you go. By me, no thanks.

A single rack, front or back, however, offers a number of advantages. It is a good mounting point for lights, and if it is on the rear and has a platform (or strip of plastic), it can help ward off road spray and grit. Depending on how clever you are at arranging and securing a load, you may be able to carry fairly heavy or awkwardly-shaped items. A very stout rack, backed up by a strong rear wheel, can carry a passenger sitting side-saddle. This is SOP in the Netherlands and throughout Asia and Africa.

Strong racks are made either of tubular steel (heavy), or of high-grade aluminium (expensive). Racks made of wire steel or cast aluminium are weaker but cost less, and can manage a light briefcase or small box.

If you have basic DIY skills, you can make a good rack for very little money. You can also utilise a design of my own invention that is better for general haulage.

Standard rear racks are designed to hold panniers closely to the bike; as a result, the top portion or load platform is too narrow to safely mount a wide load. The design solution is to forget about mounting panniers, and make the platform broad enough to support big boxes and other bulky items. For various reasons, including allowing room for the rider and structural strength, the best platform shape is a trapezoid configuration, narrow end near the bike, wide end at the rear.

Richard's creation. The rough appearance is deliberate.

How to do it? Ah. Realise, I made my rack principally of high-grade aluminium in order to have strength with lightness, because while the bike is designed to look rough (to misdirect thieves), it is in fact a swift machine with a good frame and excellent components. However, my home-built rack also includes lengths of aluminium tubing removed from a discarded ironing board found on the street.

Any recycling centre will have ample quantities of old lawn furniture and other items providing aluminium tubing in all the sizes you could ever need. The manufacturing technique is straightforward. Lay out the basic configuration using sticks and rubber bands, until you have a rough template for something that looks like it will work. Then cut aluminium tubes to size with a hacksaw or a plumber's pipe cutter. Where tubes attach to the bike, mash the ends flat with a vice or hammer, and drill holes so the ends can be bolted to the bike. You'll need to do some artistic bending and may need a few repeat tries before everything is right for size and position. Be sure to include a cross-brace, as shown in the photo. Where tubes meet tubes, you can simply bolt them together. Dimple the tubes a little (a bash with a ball-peen hammer will do it), so the bolts recess and do not protrude. Alternatively, tubes can be bound together with epoxy resin and fibreglass. At the finish, smooth any jagged or sharp edges with a file, or cover them with plastic or tape. You don't want to have a mishap yourself, or snag a luckless pedestrian when your bike is locked on the street.

A wide platform means you can carry a big box, either of whatever, or to carry other things within. There are all sorts of boxes available, some even with lids. I use a plain wood broccoli crate, because it is picturesque, and actually very lightweight. It will hold a monster sack of groceries. Or a dozen tomato plants. Things can be chucked in willy-nilly, or systematically piled and lashed until the load towers as high as my head. I do that only once in a while, however, and usually only with bulky, light things such as bog paper, because skyscraper loads tend to destabilise bike handling. When you want to cart home a weeks' worth of groceries all at once, it is time for the next option — a trailer.

Trailers are brilliant. They can carry heavy loads and, depending on model and design, an array of large and awkwardly-shaped things; other bikes, sheets of plywood, bricks and bags of cement, and what-else.

Bike-Hod

An amazing amount of stuff can be piled onto a Bike-Hod.

Most trailers attach to the bike via a quick on-off hitch, which allows for the trailer to be put aside when not in use, and for the bike to then be used purely as a bike. Another bonus is that the trailer can be used as a shopping cart, and on arrival home, wheeled straight into the kitchen for unloading.

There are three basic types of trailers: two-wheel upright, two-wheel low, and single-wheel low. A two-wheel upright trailer resembles a golf bag on wheels, or without a bag, one of those folding gizmos that can be used for trundling luggage about, and usually attaches to the seat post via a long arm and a flexible hitch, so the bike can lean while the trailer remains upright. The design is very adaptable for load carrying, and the effect on bike performance, while noticeable, is controlled.

A two-wheel low design is typically an open box or load platform with wheels on either side, and connects to the bike via a long U-shape arm hitched at the rear hub. Larger models are available which can carry one or even two children, or impressive quantities of shopping.

Low box

The single wheel design is configured long and low, and attaches to the rear hub. Depending on model, the carrying capacity can be quite good, but the strong point is performance. You can hitch one of these to a mountain bike, and still ride very rough terrain with ease and confidence. Basically, it is a design for performance touring, which can also cart home a fair load of groceries.

The drawback with trailers is cost; most models are pretty expensive. On the plus side, there is not much to go wrong and they last a long time; one of mine is 25 years old and still rolling fine.

Cargo Bikes

This may sound curious, but perhaps the nicest thing about cargo cycles is that they are a lot of fun! You've at last got something expressly made for the job. There's no more fiddling about with hitches and straps and other gear; you just put your load aboard and go. And riding is a pleasure, with good handling even with a heavy load.

Bonus: you can carry people, too. This is quite handy when you want to make a dash to catch a meal and go to the cinema.

A down side is expense. These machines are limited-production by small firms, and have price tags to match. All I can say is, I saved my pennies, and did it. Our new 8-freight will last for decades, and will be used by all the family, and friends, too.

8-Freight

Another possible down point is parking. Cargo bikes tend to be big, and need a lot of space. One solution is to simply park on the street or road (cycles are not subject to parking regulations), but this leaves the machine vulnerable to vandalism. Another solution is to look afield. If you have a regular bike, you could store the cargo bike in a garage somewhere reasonably nearby, and just ride over to fetch it.

Thought: several people and/or families could share a cargo bike. This would cut down expense.

IV: RIDING

Bike Handling Skills

Cycling is wonderfully democratic. Rich and poor, young and old — almost anyone can ride a bike. Naturally, some people are better at it than others! A fit and capable bike messenger speeding along a crowded high street functions at a different level than a dowager gently gliding on a segregated cycle path. Yet as riders, both are subject to the same dictum: the better you can handle a bike, the happier, safer and more comfortable you are.

Playing is the best way to pick up and maintain bike-handling skills. Fun is good! For a playground, find a place where you can whiz around without having to worry about cars or pedestrians: a limited-access street, an empty car park, a playground. You do not need a huge space, but it must be one in which you can relax and concentrate on exercises and drills. I like car parks, as they usually have painted lines that are useful markers for exercises. The nearer to home, the more often you will be able to play.

Basic skills

Basic skills include starting off smoothly, riding in a straight line, turning when you want, avoiding obstacles, and braking and stopping. Also, being able to look behind, and signal turns, without veering off-course.

Starting Off

Objective: start off and move up to speed with a minimum of side-to-side movement.

Why: in traffic, space is often limited. When queuing at a junction or traffic light, vehicles pack closely together and then on starting off, jostle for position at close quarters. It is no time to be wobbling about! You want a straight take-off and smooth acceleration to riding speed.

Learning to ride a bicycle is a snap. Do it by yourself. Remove the pedals and lower the saddle until you can sit on the bike with your feet flat on the ground. Find an open area without cars such as a park or large courtyard. Sit on the bike, place your hands on the bars and squeeze the brake levers firmly but not tightly. Push the bike forward with both feet. The bike should stay put, if not, squeeze the brake levers harder. OK, now release the levers a little, push with your feet, and apply the brakes again. You should move a little, then stop. That's how you start and stop. Do it several times, until you are able to stop when you want.

Next, release the brake levers, push, and go just a little distance before you stop. Again. Again. Again — each time, a little longer. OK, now push, and for a moment, lift both feet clear of the ground. Again! Leave out the stops. Whee! Next, try scooting along by alternately pushing off with one foot after the other. You are hobby-horsing, riding the way cyclists did before a bright spark (historians scrap over who it was) thought of adding pedals to a bike.

Find some open ground with a bit of gentle slope. Now you can scoot for really long distances. In fact, you can get the bike going, and then hold your feet clear of the ground. Keep on coasting until you are comfortable rolling downhill for a good distance. Then, put the pedals back on the bike. Take off from the top of the slope, and rest your feet on the pedals. Give them a spin or two if you want. When you are ready, pedal — hey, you can ride a bike!

Take off

Method: straddle the bike and place the pedal you wish to use for take-off a little forward of the top position. (If, as most people do, you tap the pedal to spin the crank backward, take care not to bark your shin.) Put your foot on the pedal, push off with the other foot and simultaneously stroke down the pedal. As the bike moves forward, use the push of the stroke to raise yourself up and back onto the saddle, and in almost the same motion, lift your other foot onto the opposite pedal as it comes up to top position and commence pedalling. You're away. The process is a matter of co-ordination, and is easily learnt with practise.

With step-in pedals, you have to push down on the pedal in order to clip in. Often, this is easier to do at the bottom of the stroke. If you have toe clips and straps (which some people prefer, because you can ride wearing ordinary shoes), then you need to learn a trick. When you take off, the weight of the toe clip and strap will hold the pedal upside down. To present the pedal right side up, tap the underside with the sole of your shoe — some models have a small tab for exactly this purpose — just hard enough to spin the pedal a half-turn so you can deftly slip your foot into the toe clip and keep on pedalling without missing a beat! It does take practise, you need to tap the pedal as it is rising to top position, but with time the process becomes pretty well automatic.

The gear ratio you use has a big effect on the smoothness of your take-off. If it is very high (hard to push), completing the first stroke will take an age, and if it is very low, the first stroke will be over before you have got yourself sorted. Another factor is gradient. For an uphill start you need to use a gear low enough to push without strain, which means you need to execute the take-off crisply. (See below for more information on gears and shifting.)

Do the take-off drill along a painted line, seeing, of course, how close you can keep to the line. Set yourself problems, such as starting in too high or too low a gear.

Starting Off II

In stop-and-go traffic, a full take-off may be too strong. An alternate method is to scoot, which is done by placing one foot on a pedal at the bottom of the stroke, and using the other foot to push along as required. One or two firm pushes will usually provide enough momentum for a take-off.

Props

I put a lot of emphasis on being able to execute a smooth take-off with a lift into the saddle, because if you are riding and have to stop, there is a temptation to look for a prop that will enable you to maintain balance while halted, without leaving the saddle. The kerb is the most common prop, and is fine to use when first starting off, as in exiting the house and entering the street or road. It is not so good at a junction or traffic light. The reason is, one has to be all the way to the left side of the lane in order to reach the kerb, and this sacrifices a central or primary position in the lane. A car can pull up alongside and then the room for a safe take-off will be dangerously tight. Or, you can be in the middle of take-off, and a car will whiz alongside with an inch to spare. You pre-empt these problems by maintaining a central position in the lane when stopping and starting. Which is why you want to be cool with no-prop starts.

Pedalling

Eh? What's to know? You push the pedals. The harder you push, the faster you go. No!

Think of the pedals as devices that connect you to the cranks. What you want to do is spin the cranks. You push on the down stroke, and as well, you actively move your foot and leg through the other parts of the complete crank rotation.

Why: muscles work through combustion; stored fuel and oxygen are burned when muscles contract. The combustion process generates waste products, such as lactic acid, which need to be washed away. Fuel and oxygen also need to be replaced. The cleaning and recharging processes both take place through blood circulation, and can happen only when the muscle is relaxed.

The time for rejuvenating a muscle is about four times longer than the period of contraction or burn. This coincides with the work and rest periods in a complete crank rotation. As well, muscles more easily manage a series of light efforts than a single heavy work-load. You can do ten light pulls and be ready for more, whereas one hard pull may spend everything you have. So in a nutshell, spinning cranks lightly is more effective than giving the pedals one monster stomp.

Spinning is best for over-all metabolic efficiency, but it is also about power. Spinning itself generates a momentum that contributes to your torque. This is not something you can feel on the first day out. But with time, as your spin gradually improves, the moment will come when you reach for more power — and it is there! It is an amazing feeling.

Exercise: gear down until there is almost no pedalling resistance and your feet can barely stay on the pedals. This is when clip-in pedals or toe clips are handy, but if you do not have — no matter. The main thing is to dance on those pedals, to whirl the cranks so fast, it is everything you can do to stay with them. Bzzzzzzzzzz!

You'll find that fairly naturally, you use a technique known as ankling, pivoting at the ankle to push down at the bottom of the stroke, and to lift up at the top of the stroke. Some people practise this sort of thing very consciously, but I wouldn't worry too much about it. Just whip those cranks around so fast, your feet are floating on the pedals.

This is not just a parking lot exercise. I start and end most rides pedalling lightly and rapidly in a low gear. At the start, the purpose is to warm up; at the end, to warm down and, in particular, to clear out the waste products from the ride.

Pedalling rate is known as cadence, and is the number of revolutions of the cranks per minute. What is the right cadence? That depends, of course. An old soak riding to the pub for a regular tipple might trundle at 40 to 50 RPM. An everyday local rider might turn 60 to 70 RPM, an experienced tourist 70 to 80 RPM. Racers run 90 RPM and up.

Using a cycle computer with a cadence function is recommended for seriously maximising engine performance. But for a simple rule of thumb, if your legs are burning, you are pushing too hard, and if you are gasping for breath, you are spinning too fast.

Shifting

The function of gears is to keep your cadence at optimum rate, hence on road racing bikes the gear ratios are closely spaced together and little different from each other. General use bikes have more widely spaced gear ratios, and touring and mountain bikes typically have wide-ratio gears.

With hub gears, options are limited. You can go up or down through the gears, and in many cases, there will be no overlap; each ratio will be different.

If you have derailleur gears, you'll find that ratios overlap, and also, that you can achieve the same ratio, or nearly so, with different combinations of chain rings (front) and sprockets (rear). OK, now, very briefly, as you gain experience, you will find which gear ratios and shift patterns you like best. Out on the open road, you may well enjoy executing double-alpine shifts and other fancy moves for fun. In traffic, you likely will want to keep the moves simple.

At this stage I have just a couple of points to make. One: for both derailleur and hub gear systems, at the moment you shift, reduce pedalling pressure while the chain moves to another chain ring or sprocket, or the gear changes. Two: with derailleur systems, keep the chain line reasonably straight. That means, in particular, never run the chain from the smallest chain ring to the smallest sprocket, nor from the biggest chain ring to the biggest sprocket. However, :-)!, if you have three chain rings, you can run from the middle chain ring to any of the rear sprockets. Often, this all you ever need for town riding.

Straight-line Tracking

You want to be able to lay down a smooth, straight track. This is an easy one to practise, because there are paint lines everywhere. Just get on a line,

Clockwise from top left:

Chain on large sprocket at rear and small chain ring at front gives a low gear and easier pedalling. For hills.

Chain on small sprocket at rear and large chain ring at front gives a high gear and harder pedalling. For speed.

If the chain is on a small sprocket at the rear, it should be on the large or middle chain ring at the front. If the chain is on the middle chain ring, any of the rear sprockets can be used.

and see if you can keep your wheels on the paint. Do this only in dry conditions, as when wet, paint lines are slippery. You'll quickly discover that you need to pedal smoothly, and that even light pressure on the handlebars affects the steering.

Ok, now take one hand off the handlebars. Why? Because you need to be able to maintain a straight track while signalling, fishing out a water-bottle, waving to a friend, turning around to look for UFOs behind, or whatever. You'll find that riding with one hand, you have to apply slightly different pressure to the handlebar.

Looking Behind

Looking behind is an important skill. How you do it depends on your bike riding position, and on your physique.

The classic technique is to sit upright, remove one hand from the handlebars (in the UK, usually the right), and dangle the arm to the side while twisting the head and torso for a look behind. It sounds a bit of a production, and is. I generally do it only when I want to be obviously looking at someone in order to command their attention, for example a motorist whose consciousness is deep inside a mobile telephone.

A faster method for looking behind can be used if your riding position is one where you lean forward and carry some of your weight with your hands and arms. Both hands remain on the bars, and the head is ducked forward and only partly twisted. It is almost, but not quite, an upside-down look. If necessary, one arm can be dropped.

You can fit a rear-view mirror, either to a bike, or to your helmet or glasses. Mirrors are useful, definitely, but are not good enough to bet your life on. You need a direct look, too. However, on a recumbent bike, a mirror is essential. When riding a recumbent trike I sometimes look rearward by tilting my head backward and a little to one side. The image is upside-down but still has the information I need.

Signalling

Signal all your turns, always, and stops when you have traffic around you. For a turn, stick the appropriate arm out at a right angle to your body. For a stop, stick your arm out and make a continuous downward patting motion. Obvious, sure, but practise these moves in your play area. As you will learn, signalling is one of the ways you can take charge of, and sort out, a difficult situation in traffic. It is just at such moments that you might want to clutch the handlebars with both hands, hence the need to be utterly confident riding with one hand. So play! I sometimes pretend my signal hand is a flasher, and then on a flash let my hand and arm lead into the turn as the bike heels over – almost as a dance movement.

Picking A Path

It is important to be able to go exactly where you want. Use paper, tape, leaves or something harmless (to you) to mark a gap, say, a foot wide to start. Whiz through it, straight on and from the side, at varying speeds. Tighten up the gap. With practise, you will be able to narrow it down to a tyre-width.

Turning

Most turns happen naturally; the bike leans and around you go. If you need to initiate a turn quickly, push the inside handlebar end away from you (or pull the outside handlebar end toward you). The bike will heel right over. To pick it up straight again, pull the inside handlebar end (or opposite, for outside bar end). Careful with this manoeuvre, because just a light push or pull can make a bike really jump. As with hard braking, haul handlebar or dive turns are something to practise in a park or unused parking lot.

In a steep turn, when the bike is leaning far over, stop pedalling and keep the inside pedal up and the outside pedal down and trailing back just a bit. Shift more weight to the outside pedal. This will help centre the weight down low. Wait until you are past the apex of the turn and the bike is coming back up before pedalling again. Obviously, you wish to avoid grounding an inside pedal. The degree of lean before contact is made depends on the particular pedal; some ground easily, others are designed for more clearance. Five words: always allow plenty of room.

It is possible to manoeuvre a bike around underneath you, for example, to use the handlebars to push the bike down into a steeper angle of lean, while your torso still remains relatively upright. This can be useful if you need to tighten up a turn.

Alternatively, you can throw a bike more upright, but lower your body deeper into a turn. The idea here is to lighten up the lateral (sideways) force in corner, so as to not, for example, lose traction on a slippery or gravel surface. It can also help reduce the shock of a bump or rough surface.

Avoid braking in corners; it can cost traction and control. If you must brake, favour the rear brake. Loss of traction will result in a slide and a dump, not a happy experience, but better than the lightning-fast hard smash which happens when a front wheel washes out. But you will avoid these problems by braking before you enter corners, eh?

Overcooking

What do you do if you overcook a corner and find yourself heading off the road? The first problem here is panic: I'm gonna crash! causes you freeze tight, whereupon you do indeed sail off-course. You cure this in advance in your play sessions by finding out just how hard you can turn, and how to recover a turn which is in danger of becoming lost.

A bike can heel over at a steeper angle than most people ever want to go. The limit here isn't the bike, it is you. Set up a course with two to three turns and run it faster and faster until you reach your limit. Heads up: this exercise is not a test of nerve! What you want to do is slowly stretch and extend your limit.

OK, now, for recovering an over-cooked turn (you went in too fast), there are two options. The first is: muscle the bike into a steeper angle of lean. You do this with handlebar pressure, pressing down with the outside knee, and pivoting from the outside foot. Naturally, you are going to practise this in your nice, safe play area, so if you do truly over-cook and run wide, there will be no harm done.

Option two definitely requires experience. The fastest line or path through a corner does not exactly follow the radius of the turn, but rather, starts high or wide, cuts to the inside at the apex, and then runs wide again on exit. If you are going too fast, it may be possible to throw the bike upright and brake very hard, and then dive the bike back down again to make what will be a sharper turn, but at reduced speed. This manoeuvre works better with longer, faster corners, and again, is one that by golly, you must practise in a play area before trying to use it for real!

Obstacles

You can go around or over obstacles. Going around, say, a rock, is haul- (or push-) handlebar in fast time. You give the bars a hard, fast tweak, and the bike moves out from under you and tracks around the rock. Of course, the bike is now unhinged, you need to catch up with each other on the other side, by tweaking the bars again, the opposite way. Ho-ho, this manoeuvre is another one to learn slowly and practise with care.

Jumping an obstacle is sometimes the only available option, for example when you unexpectedly meet a pot-hole and have no time or room to veer around it. Stand up a bit, press down with your feet and hands as if to bounce, and then rise up, rotating the bike forward as you do so. Sounds weird, but it works; the manoeuvre is known as a bunny hop. Again, you'll need to practise, and if the technique does not come easily, don't fret. It is easier for some people and harder for others.

Skilled riders can clear 50 cm

> ## CRASH!
>
> Unless you are reckless, the chances of taking a fall while practising manoeuvres in a play area are very small. The point is to gently stretch your capacities, while staying well within what the bike can do. Nonetheless, if you should fall, in practise or while on the road, stop and take the time to check both yourself and your bike for injuries. A crash can produce a massive adrenaline charge. This is a survival mechanism exactly designed to keep you going despite injuries. All too often, one can be misled into thinking 'I'm all right', when that may not be the case.
>
> Crash, first thing, check yourself carefully. Take the time to register how you are feeling, and if anything seems to be off. Breathe a little, stroke your arms and legs to check for bruises or cuts, and pause to put yourself in charge. Second thing, inspect the bike, and be thorough. It is easily possible for something to have been damaged, without the harm being obvious.
>
> When you and the bike check A-OK, go again.

Fast Stops

When you brake a bike, your weight moves forward. The front wheel has more traction, and hence more braking power. Conversely, the rear wheel has less weight and less traction and is more inclined to lock up and skid.

For a rapid stop you shift your body weight rearward while applying the front brake as strongly as possible without causing the bike to cartwheel and also applying the rear brake just firmly enough to provide braking power without locking up and skidding. This is absolutely something you must practise! For safety and effective learning, do the moves slowly at first. Develop a feeling for the dynamics involved before you try fast stops.

Fast Stop

Throw body rearward, keep weight centred on pedals, and don't forget to kiss.

The moves: at the moment you want to stop, increase weight on the pedals and throw your posterior straight rearward, almost clear of the saddle. This puts your weight back and centred down low, through the pedals. At the same time as you shift rearward, apply both brakes, the front firmly and with increasing pressure, the rear also firmly but less so, and ready to lighten pressure ('feather') on the lever if the rear wheel locks up.

Slowly at first! Modern cycle brakes are strong. Over-zealous application of the front brake can cause a bike to cartwheel and dash you head-first to the ground. Concentrate not on speed, but on getting the moves right. One-two-three. One-two-three. Once you have a feel for what is happening, pick a braking point, and start tightening up the distance for a stop. Again, don't rush. Always maintain control.

You should now notice that there is a lot of steering effect from how you press on the pedals. In fact, an old mountain biking technique is to lock up the back wheel, and steer the bike with a combination of pressures on the pedals and handlebars. Locking up the back end and sliding around is not the fastest way to stop, but (so long as you are comfortable with the move) do it anyhow, to develop a feel for controlling a skidding bike, and for sensing the point at which you need to feather the rear brake in order to maintain traction.

OK? Cool? Now see how short you can cut the distance for a stop. You'll need to stop balanced, both feet still on the pedals, and then disengage a foot to touch the ground. Watch this one, it is possible to disengage one pedal, and then discover you are toppling to the opposite side!

You'll need several sessions to develop a good level of skill, and thereafter should practise regularly. On my rides I usually give the brakes a good firm pull as a safety check when starting out, and on returning home, sometimes do an all-out stop right in front of the house, cutting it as fine as possible. It wrings the bike a bit, and may even burn rubber, but the exercise keeps me wired; when I do have to pull a fast, unexpected stop in traffic, my body reacts automatically, without need for thought or instruction.

The Innermost Secrets Of Speed And Happiness!

Traffic is a dynamic environment. To ride in it efficiently and happily, you must be aware, fluid, and adaptable. Of course, traffic is also very physical, and so are many riding techniques. For examples, specific signals are used to indicate turns, and cyclists can ride centre-lane when they want to block following vehicles from overtaking.

However, simply following established forms and procedures for riding will sometimes leave you behind the actual pace of events and make you feel uncertain and uncomfortable. Traffic constantly shifts and changes. To be genuinely confident and happy when riding in traffic, you have to know when moves are going to work, and when something else is called for. Beginner or experienced veteran, what matters most for riding in traffic is understanding the general principles involved.

You Are A Vehicle

A cyclist is a vehicle. A vehicle requires space. Your space is the immediate area around you, the distance in front and behind needed for a stop, and crucially, all the places you can go. How you ride, and the way you inter-act with other road users and vehicles, delineates your space.

Your space is inviolate! You must always have your space! You cannot move or function unless you have space! I'm exclaiming, bang! bang! bang! because this point is truly essential. You ride in such a way as to always maintain your space. If your space evaporates or is taken away, through your fault or act of whatever, you bail out!

Space management: you are riding on a two-way street wide enough for cars to overtake you without changing lane. The street is flat and straight, with no junctions or speed bumps, so the motor vehicles are moving smartly. Everyone is happy, but up ahead a parked car has created a chicane, a space too narrow for a car and cycle to go side-by-side. You have to enter the lane being used by the cars. You pick your opening, signal and move over, and hold your position in the lane until the obstruction is behind and it is safe to shift left and let the cars overtake again.

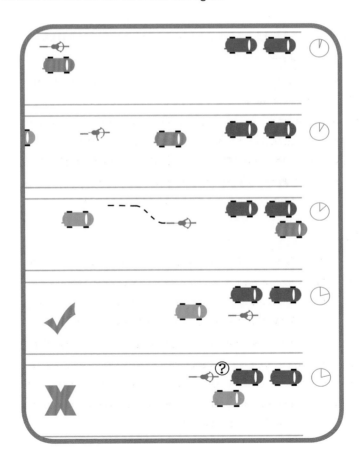

A cyclist is a vehicle, and as such, is entitled to space. Of course, it may seem that a big HGV or bus will have a lot less trouble taking and holding space than a little cyclist. OK, here is your first secret: relative to size, a cyclist has more space-defining power than any other vehicle on the road!

Stay on my wheel ... [1]

Muscle

Traffic is a series of conflicts resolved by agreements. Simple words, deep meaning and wide range of possibilities. Let's go back to that nice, straight road where you are running along at a good clip, with motor vehicles overtaking without having to shift lane. Ahead, another bottleneck. This time, it is a combination traffic island/kerb jut-out that a road engineer installed to make life easier for pedestrians, but not cyclists. You need to break into the line of overtaking motor vehicles. You signal a right lane change and

» a slightly nervous lady driver in a hatchback says, 'Oh, good, the cyclist will go first' and slows to give you room. She is relieved that the conflict is solved.

» white van man in a hurry says 'F***ing cyclist!' and surges alongside to cut you off. You are forced to brake, and now the situation quickly worsens. You are rapidly nearing the traffic island, and trying to keep an

---

[1] 'On my wheel' is a term from racing and fast riding. At 20 MPH, about 80 per cent of a rider's effort is devoted solely to overcoming air resistance. When one cyclist follows closely behind another, he or she is partially within the slipstream of the lead cyclist, and does not have to work as hard. The technique is called drafting, and is a central element of road racing tactics. Groups of riders mount surprise jumps and spurts in an effort to break away from the main pack. I still remember, at one of my first lunches with a group of racers in a noisy sausage-and-mash south London cafe, Gary Smith of F.W. Evans saying: 'First thing I learned, if you get on someone's wheel, stay there!'

eye on that while looking for an opening in the traffic flow. However, you are losing speed and hence the ability to merge smoothly. Unbeknownst to you, white van man crowding alongside has made you invisible to a motorist following (too) closely behind the van. Suddenly . . . the traffic island is there! Desperate, you brake hard and pull out behind the van, clearing it by inches. Your speed is gone and you are still a high gear that is hard to move, so you are stranded in the middle of the lane — and the car that was following too closely behind the van is right on top of you! There's an almighty screech of brakes and tyres, and . . .

Someone from the ring of wide-eyed listeners around the camp-fire urgently asks 'What happened?'

You smile and say 'I died.'

Actually, I didn't. I bailed out long ago, by hitting the brakes and stopping, because I well understood that I had completely screwed up. Remember? No space = bail out!

Commercial van drivers are notorious for being aggressive and ruthless. IT WAS MY RESPONSIBILITY to have seen that white van man was there, and to have ensured he was not in a position to bully me. If that meant coming to a complete stop, so be it. Never ride on mercy!

Anticipate!

Ride ahead of yourself. Project ahead as far as you can see, and to the extent of your knowledge. This will give you good time in which to make decisions and execute moves while maintaining your speed and space. Van man in hurry cannot box you in if you move first and pre-empt the lane space. However, this may not be your coolest move, because van man may then spitefully sit on your tail just to upset you. Better to see the obstruction from a long ways off, check behind and note the presence of van man, and to adjust your pace so that you merge either well ahead of van man, or behind him.

Smoothness

There is another principle at work here. You are looking to keep up an even, steady pace. Cars are fast but are big and often motionless because they have no space in which to move. Bikes are slower but are small and agile and can keep moving even in dense traffic.

You work with this. Your aim is to move smoothly, not rocket forward and then have to brake. That is a fierce waste of energy.

When I was learning to drive a car on public roads, my father would put a full glass of water on the dashboard of the car and say 'OK, Richard, next 100 miles, spill not a drop'. It was a technique learnt from my grandfather, a professional race car driver. Hard braking and fast starts were out. Every corner had to be a study in grace. Eventually, I could do it. What I learned was to look ahead. Way, way far ahead. I never looked very much at what was going on right in front of my nose, because that had all been decided. What mattered was the next sequence down the line, and the one after that.

One of the core secrets of speed is incredibly simple: you move at speed! On a bike, 'fast' may be a steady 15 MPH, not warp velocity, but the trick is to keep it up. For exactly this reason, sometimes the fast path is to slow down just a little, so that something ahead — a traffic signal, a cross-turning vehicle, or whatever — can work out or process to give you a clear run.

Compared to a car, you have an enormous advantage, because your stop-start space is very small. Let me explain. When the M25 London ring road is very crowded, the traffic can be made to move faster by reducing the speed limit from 70 MPH to 50 MPH. What happens is, at 70 MPH, the cars surge ahead and then have to brake. The signal to brake is passed down the line from vehicle to vehicle, and each time, there is a driver reaction time before braking begins. As a result, each successive vehicle has to brake just a little harder (to make up for the distance lost in reaction time), and eventually, one car has to put out all anchors and the traffic flow comes to a complete halt. By lowering the speed limit there is less forward surge and less subsequent tail-back.

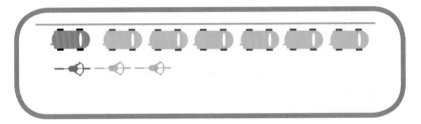

A bike only goes a short distance before being able to manoeuvre. A car uses invisible space: at 30MPH it will travel 6 car lengths before stopping.

Why? At 70 MPH, the space requirements for coping with reaction times and braking are very large. Visualise invisible spaces in front of and behind a car. The faster the speed the bigger the invisible spaces. When the invisible spaces of cars overlap, braking and eventual tail-backs and stops are inevitable. It happens on motorways, and also in dense urban traffic, where the pace is slower, but vehicles are right on top of each other. On a bicycle, at 15 MPH, there is a lot of room, and especially if you are savvy enough to drop your speed by 1 or 2 MPH at the right moments.

Now, mix pace and space, in that bikes are small and slim and can go where other vehicles cannot. For example: you are riding on a two-way street, parked cars on your left. Vehicles are overtaking, pulling out just slightly into the opposite direction lane to do so. Up ahead is a junction with a traffic light just gone red. The cars in your direction of travel are slowing and starting to touch their brakes. From behind you, Johnny Balls-Up in a tricked-out GT Whizzer TI with decorative lights and an extra-loud exhaust (silencer) system starts to overtake, only to find, of course, that the cars are stopping. He has to brake hard, and to avoid being stuck out in the middle of the road, moves back into the lane too early, cutting you off.

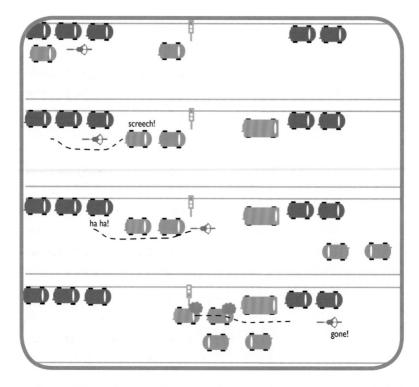

It would have happened that way but you, clever and aware soul, had heard the loud pipes on the Whizzer and foreseen Johnny's foolishness. In fact, you slowed down enough to send Johnny ahead and give you enough room to pull out behind him and into the centre of the lane, the primary position from which you have more space options (and which you pretty much always take when things are tight). Now, as the line of traffic halts, you are able to take advantage of your slim profile to swing out to the centre of the road and overtake all of the cars stopped for the light in a single run. You arrive at the head of the queue and move over the left with time to spare before the light changes to green. At the off, you make a good start, clear a stopped bus, and are a good half-mile down the road while Johnny Balls-Up, loud pipes and all, is still stuck behind the bus.

Go smooth, go fast. To learn smoothness, a simple exercise: stay off your brakes. This is clearly impractical on a downhill leading to a junction, or when a stop is required. But as an exercise, it can teach you a fantastic amount about how to read traffic and understand what will happen next.

Sprinting

Sometimes the best way to maintain pace is to sprint, to catch a green traffic signal, merge into a lane of traffic before a bus pulls alongside, or whatever. If you are reasonably fit, you should be able to hold 20 MPH for at least a short distance. Naturally, if you are young and strong, you will have more vigorous and longer-lasting suds than old-timers such as myself, who depend more on savvy and cunning than winding up the cranks.

Sprinting and catching breaks is one of the great games you can play in traffic. Take care, because it is seductive! What happens is, you are rolling along on a familiar journey route and up ahead, see a traffic light change green. You stand on the pedals, knowing that if you hustle, you will catch the light. You do, and your little burst has you moving faster than usual in the next stretch of your route. Aware that the traffic released by the light you have just cleared will be coming up from behind, you continue to stand on it and come flying down the road to the next junction just as the traffic signal changes to green. You pause momentarily to double-check that there are no red-light running motorists or laggard pedestrians, but still, you go through the junction at speed . . . and up ahead, spot a stopped bus, with four or five passengers about to board. If you hit the pedals again, you can take the bus!

Your blood is well up, and you don't even think — you're out of the saddle and gone! Me . . . puff, puff . . . I'm gonna take a breather.

If you know what you are doing, you can use catching breaks in traffic as a form of interval training. This consists (simplified) of going at a fast pace for say, 400 m, going all-out for 200 m, slowing to fast for 400 m, going all-out again for 200 m, and so on. Intervals are quite sapping; by the time you've done a half-dozen, you usually have tunnel vision and wonder where you are.

The beauty of traffic-jamming is that you work and play with your skill at understanding traffic, as well as bringing on your full juice! This is when you are all there and everything else — your troubles, and the things you should or shouldn't be doing — disappear.

For many of the people who ride bikes every day for a living, fast riding in traffic is a transcendental experience. One way to be safe in traffic is to be faster than anything else. You see spaces before they exist, and are part of them as they happen. Evolved bike couriers ride lean, stripped-down machines with every affinity to fine time-trial and racing bikes. A courier with highly refined sensibilities and strong legs can carve out an urban journey that is simply awesome. The pace and mastery are so great, it seems like floating above the traffic.

Whoa — all in good time, eh? You can aspire to developing muscles of spring steel and the riding skills to be a lord of urban creation, but mind Bruce Lee's advice and stretch your capabilities a bit at a time. The danger in fast traffic-jamming is becoming over-extended and taking chances in order to stay on the pace. You'll know when this happens, and when it does, slow down and take a break! Remember, the game is about mastery and control. Reduce that, and you reduce your space — a no-no.

BALLANTINE'S SEVENTH LAW OF LOOKOUT!

Car brakes are better than cycle brakes! Never tailgate. You want plenty of space between you and any vehicle you are following, and herein lies a recurring problem for cyclists.

Most motorists are unaware that grace and smoothness yield greater speed. Instead of holding back, they push and crowd, and when there is a space ahead the size of a car, they often try to get into it. As a result, if you are riding in traffic and allow a sensible space between yourself and the vehicle ahead, brain-off motorists will attempt to overtake you and slot into the space you need for yourself.

You prevent inappropriate overtaking by a combination of riding tight on your front space, and holding the centre of your lane so overtaking is not possible. A cycle is very manoeuvrable and so long as there is some kind of escape path available, you can crowd your front space. However, there is a limit, and if a motorist is pushing hard enough from behind, the best course may be to let them by.

It's OK. You are actually faster! And anyway, best to keep unskilled and immature motorists in front of you, where you can keep an eye on them.

Position

In real estate, the main factors are location, location, and location. In traffic, it is position, position, and position! Your placement is the key to defining where you can go, and hence the extent of your space.

What lies ahead is far more important than what might come from astern. Cyclists tend to be apprehensive about being hit by vehicles from behind, but rear-end crashes account for just five per cent of bike/car collisions; the majority are frontal crashes at turns and junctions. One reason this happens is: out of fear of being hit from behind, many cyclists ride too far to the left and thereby are less visible to traffic ahead.

Mobbed Up

Rush hour, crowded traffic, and these cyclists are rightly using weight of numbers to take full possession of a lane.

Alone in a churning sea of vehicles, the lone cyclist is doing exactly the right thing: holding centre-lane, and control.

By riding too far to the left this cyclist has lost control of his space and is about to be hemmed in by a bus.

Do not be scared to take your rightful place on the road! It is much safer than trying to hide! Your rightful place is in the centre of the lane. This is where everyone can most readily see you, and this is the platform, or space, from which you have the greatest possible number of paths for forward movement. It is also the best position for control of following and overtaking vehicles.

Standard advice for cyclists is to not ride in the gutter, but to stay to the left 'as far as is safe'. Real meaning: do what you can to stay out of the way. This is the wrong perspective. Always take the best position for you.

» You're on a two-way street running into a cross-junction. There are parked cars, and single lanes of traffic in each direction. You ride bang in the centre of your lane, well clear of a possible opening door on a parked car, and fully controlling the vehicle behind you. You have maximum visibility to the various other vehicles in, or about to enter, the junction.

» You're on a two-way street running into a cross-junction. There are no parked cars, and single lanes of traffic in each direction. There is enough room for you to ride to the left and allow cars to overtake. Do you? NO! The most important thing is that you be seen by the vehicles already in, or about to enter, the junction.

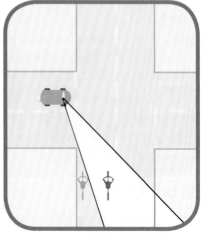

Be seen

Cyclist riding near kerb is invisible to motorist about to cross junction. Cyclist riding centre-lane is in better shape.

» You're on a two-way street. There are occasional parked cars, and a few other interesting problems, such as pedestrian traffic islands, and big buses. This is a little trickier, because you have to balance the courtesy of allowing motorists to overtake by riding to the left, and the problems you will have re-joining the flow of traffic around parked cars, etc.

One element is your speed. On a climb, you won't be moving very fast, and it is harder to break into a lane of faster traffic. On a descent, or if you are whistling along at a good clip on your own legs, you can more easily move in and out of a lane of fast traffic.

At this stage, a couple of other main principles come into play: Communication, and Reading Traffic.

Communication

You are very visible, and far better able to communicate with other road users than a motorist nestled within a car. Let's take the example of a lane change. You can signal, and at the same time, look directly at the driver of the vehicle you are proposing to move in front of. You can see if the driver sees you, and if all is well with celestial aspects and said motorist's love life, when you signal and catch their eye, they will usually give you a small indication — perhaps a flip of the hand or nod of the head — for you to go ahead and make your move. It takes lots longer to write about than to happen, and indeed, in this kind of give-and-take communication, it is important that you respond and act on resolutions without delay. Remember, traffic is a series of conflicts resolved by agreements. The quicker and more clearly agreements are made, the happier everyone is. More, much more, on communication in a bit.

Reading Traffic

Here, there is an awful lot to talk about. First thing to say up front is, your ability to read traffic will depend a lot on your experience. If you have never driven a motorcycle, car, lorry, or bus, your understanding of the particular problems of each of these types of vehicles will be limited. This is no crime, lots of people do not have driving licenses, but if you are in this category, realise you have a lot of learning to do.

Traffic is people. Pedestrians, dogs, cats, wayward urchins, and low-flying geese aside, your primary focus is on other vehicles, all of which are under human control. You see the vehicle but how it behaves is down to the driver.

Traffic is people is feelings! I can often tell with a glance which vehicles are going to get into trouble. A certain way of pulling out, of crowding another motorist too closely, or any of a thousand and one clues, and sure enough, there goes the car that, at the next junction, pushes through on the amber and very nearly clips another car that blindly started a cross-turn on the light-change without looking to see what sort of nut-case might be coming toward them. Each driver curses the other, and each is wrong.

Important: most crashes are due to driver error. The root source of that error is almost invariably emotional.

Driving is a matter of vehicle-handling skill, of course, but heaven spare me people who say they can drive! They are never, ever as good as they think they are. Driving is physical ability, but more, it is maturity in judgement and behaviour, and comprehensive awareness of all that is happening.

As a cyclist in traffic, you need to be good because you have to be. You have your shirt for protection. Yon motorist is shrouded in armour-plating, cosseted by a seat-belt and air-bags, and can afford to be sloppy. Or take chances. As a cyclist, you cannot; you must be a better 'driver' in the sense of more fully understanding what is happening.

That is a tall order. How do you learn everything you need to know?

Well, one rather good technique is suggested by John Franklin in his book *Cyclecraft*: go out to a busy road junction, make yourself comfortable, and observe. Initially, it may feel like watching paint dry. As it were, stay on wheel. You will see that some vehicles move through the junction easily and smoothly, while others move jerkily or even violently. Observe for long enough, and you will start to identify which kinds of vehicles and drivers are apt to have trouble, or enjoy easy passage.

Some vehicles are intrinsically ill-behaved and dangerous. Skip-lorries, for example. The reason is, drivers are paid per delivery, and this makes them aggressive. Skip-lorry drivers often run full throttle, and charge full-tilt through tight spaces with inches to spare. There is a real skill involved, but it is grievously misapplied . . . skip-lorries are known, confirmed killers of pedestrians and cyclists. They are absolutely dangerous. Which means, simply, you give these critters a wide berth!

Bull Bars

Bull bars increase the severity of crash injuries to pedestrians and cyclists.

The time is 3 to 4 in the afternoon and along comes Hyper Annie Super Mom, nipping four kids home from school. For the sake of safety, Hyper Annie has a huge SUV with big bull bars front and rear. This is counter-productive, because Hyper Annie has poor vehicle handling skills and worse eyesight (she is too vain to admit she needs eyeglasses), and is frightened by the ungainly bulk of her SUV. Her fear, and the distractive yammering and chattering of the kids, makes her tense and rigid. She hopes that by blindly forging ahead, she can just get the whole thing over with. Hyper Annie Super Mom is aggressive by reason of incompetence rather than exercise of skill, but she, too, is a killer.

The common characteristic of dangerous drivers is inflated self-importance.

Grrrrrr!

Back On the Road

So there we are again, that same darn two-way street with a few odd parked cars and other obstacles, and a steady stream of overtaking motor vehicles. If there were no parked cars, you would run a little to the left, and the motor vehicles would overtake at will. But in the course of, say, a quarter-mile or so, you will need to be in the same lane as the cars, three or four times.

A lot of things happen all at once. All along, you have been keeping track of the traffic, both ahead and behind. You are stopped at a junction, there are three cars alongside, and then a C11 bus. Ah . . . C11 buses are mean. The reason is that their route is through narrow streets, and the drivers can make progress only if they crowd and push at every opportunity.

The lead car in the queue on your right side is signalling a right turn, and across the junction there are two cars waiting to come in the opposite direction. This means the cars on your side will be held up for a few moments behind the right-turning car until the junction clears, so on the off, you go swiftly, move around the mid-junction blockage to the centre of the main lane, and hold your position until you pass two parked cars. Then you move left and let the traffic overtake. If you had dawdled on the off, you would not have made it over into centre-lane, and if you had moved over left after the first parked car, you would have been boxed in by a continuous stream of overtaking vehicles.

Problems are not yet over, up ahead is another parked car. By now, mean old C11 bus is well by. You sit up and take a good look behind. Ooops, right behind is a car with the driver lost inside a mobile phone, no chance of attention there, but next in line is a black cab. You catch the driver's eye, and with your forearm slightly bent and the palm of your hand flat, you jab outward with a emphatic motion which means: 'I want to/am going there'.

The cabbie nods, and right on that motion you change lane, your signal hand now showing an upraised thumb of thanks, and since the cabbie was nice, you bend the pedals and keep up a good turn of speed past the parked car. As soon as you are clear, you swoop left to let the cabbie by.

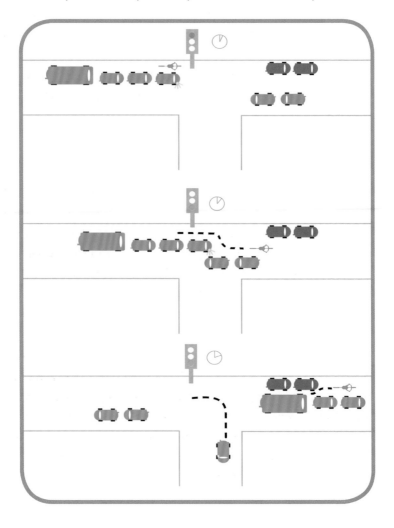

That was a simple one, too. I haven't even talked about all of the scanning you were doing, to look ahead for pot-holes and rocks, and everywhere for kids and dogs and what-else. Nor your consciousness that still further ahead, the C11 bus has stopped to take on passengers.

A human being is a fantastic piece of kit, far more complex and capable than any computer made. You may not believe the number of things you can take on board at once. The thing about riding well in traffic is that it is fun! The trick, of course, is to bite off what you can chew, and to always respect that you are on a learning curve with a good deal of length and depth. And when you miscalculate, to bail!

Flexibility

I'm on my way home from the dentist, riding north on a one-way, two-lane street that ends in a T-junction with a major east-west arterial route, three lanes each way, separated by a big divider. There is a traffic light, and vehicles on my street have two simple options: left lane turns left and westbound, and right lane goes across the big road and divider and turns right and eastbound. Normally, I go right and eastbound, because it is then easy to hang a left at the park and follow a ring road around to my neighbourhood.

Problem: traffic on the street has been royally screwed up by a half-dozen traffic wardens, who have double-parked their van near the junction, causing the two lines of traffic queuing for the signal to conflict and pinch. There is no room in the right lane. I go up the inside on the left side of the street and force a way around the van, muttering 'Poor parking' to a traffic warden. My plan is to get back to the right lane. If I go left and westbound, then I will need to filter across three lanes of heavy, fast traffic in order to turn right onto a northbound street and proceed into the park. Likely, I would have to bail out.

The light changes before I reach the junction, the queued traffic moves off smartly, and there is no chance to shift to the right lane. But there is ample room on the inside of the left turn, and so I change plan and accelerate and come through the bend and out onto the multi-lane road with a good head of speed. In for a penny, in for pound. As luck has it, traffic on the main road is sorting out, and there is an opening. On my right there are two E-class Mercedes cars, one in each lane, each with chauffeur drivers who in response to my firm signal, give me just that moment I need to sweep across the road to the right side of the right lane. I rolling-stop pause for a traffic signal, then move quickly down the road and filter right into a holding lane for a right turn, keeping to the left side of the lane in order to stay out of the way of following vehicles and at the same time be set up in the correct lane for a left turn at the park, and a run along the other half of the ring road to home turf.

It all happened in seconds. I knew the territory and could make an instant decision for major change of route, had the experience and muscle to deal with lane-changing across a multi-lane road, and in the E-class Mercs with professional drivers, a touch of serendipity, too. And if all this chemistry had not worked out, I was ready to bail.

Courtesy

Expediting the passage of others will help you! When all players in a traffic scene strive for grace and harmony, movement is smoother and quicker. The more active your role, the greater your importance as a player. The more you help others, the more you will be helped.

You are proceeding along a street. There is a cross-junction, with a car from the opposite direction stopped and waiting to make a turn across your path. You can see the driver of the car sees you, and it is evident that she is uncertain if she can make the turn ahead of you (she is jabbing the brakes and nosing ahead in small lurches, her head is tilted and eyes are slanted to the side, and her lips are pinched). You are aware that 25 or 30 metres behind you is a following car, which means that if the cross-turning car does not turn in front of you, it will be stuck in place for a while. There is a real danger that this will lead Ms Uncertain driver to make the wrong decision, and pull out in front of you.

You help out. You sit more erect in the saddle, slow a little, and wave Ms Uncertain through. Relieved, she hits the throttle and clears the junction. You, and the car behind, proceed without sweat or apprehension. Indeed, as you clear a parked car and then tuck in left and wave the following car on by, the driver gives you a just slightly ironic smile and return wave. He has understood and co-operated with the whole sequence of events. Perhaps he is a cyclist, too.

Congratulations. You are an active road citizen. By engaging in discourse for ongoing events, you assume a larger role and greater importance. Communication is one of your greatest assets. Equally, lack of communication is a red-flag danger signal.

I seriously dislike telephone-using motorists. They are complete twerps. Their limited attention and consciousness are elsewhere, instead of being focused on something far more important: ME! There is nothing so dismaying as riding along a street and spotting a car ahead waiting to enter the street, with the driver

looking the other way while yak-king on a phone. The danger is acute, and unless and until the driver sees me, I slow down and position away from the vehicle. If there are vehicles behind me, I signal elaborately that I am slowing, and then in the fashion of a lead rider who points to pot-holes, King Cobras and other hazards for the benefit of following riders, proceed slowly around the stopped vehicle while grandstand-pointing at the twerp. There is some possibility the offending motorist will notice and perhaps even be humiliated, but the principal purpose of this histrionic is to explain to the drivers of following vehicles that I have slowed for a danger hazard.

Cyclists' Rage!

There is a lot you can do to make cycling in traffic fun and enjoyable. Still, conflict is an innate feature of traffic, and sometimes the friction is raw and abrasive. Often, when a motorist is careless or aggressive, your only practical course is to give way. Your priority is to stay alive. A steady diet of this sort of thing has a bad effect on your psyche. No one thrives on being abused and pushed around. Just the opposite. You can become hostile and prone to over-react with extreme and even hysterical anger — cyclists' rage.

I cannot tell you how to change within so that you grow and become enlightened and never troubled by things such as motorists abusing and endangering you. Threats to your life are infuriating. However, I can tell you for sure that expressing rage rarely promotes your safety or well being. Anger directed against a sinner motorist produces polarisation, not conversion. The stupid become dumber, and the mean become nastier.

All of my friends who are long-term cyclists say the same thing: the best defence against idiocy and outrageous misbehaviour is humour. That's fine, I do my best to make sarcastic comments when called for. More fundamentally, when something goes badly, I ask myself how I could have done better and prevented the problem from happening. The advantage of this approach, as opposed to having a go at a motorist, is that improvement is attainable.

There is a tricky balance to be maintained. I am a great advocate of assertive cycling. I do not think you should take any guff at all. For example, on a narrow two-way street when a motorist and cyclist are converging head-on, a common occurrence is for the motorist to run centre-lane, rather than keeping to the left and allowing good room for the cyclist. When this happen to me, I move centre-lane, too. What happens next depends on who is playing. A reasonable motorist will understand you are advertising your presence and move over left, whereupon you do the same. Hyper Annie in a big SUV may take no notice of an inconsequential cyclist and charge on regardless. You do the same, and usually, Hyper Annie suddenly comes to her senses and shifts left. Aggressive drivers, such as white van man or junior hot stuff or mini-cab Dan, may welcome a game of chicken! They do not mind if you get hurt. Do not play with these types unless you enjoy hard confrontation, and have a safe escape route.

Putting It All Together

I started cycling in New York City, in the days when conditions for two-wheel transport were anarchistic and lawless. Cyclists were an aberrant form of life. You survived on your own steam or not at all. This made me an aggressive rider, and when I started writing books about cycling, created funny dilemmas. I would scribe something belligerent such as: 'When a motorist gives you the horn, give them the finger!' and then suddenly think: 'This for a 55 year old grandmother?' And: 'Hang on — some people are gentle and not into confrontation.'

Time has moved on. I continue to have an image in my head of a kindly, 55-year-old white-haired grandmother who should not have to contend with mean motorists, but I myself am now 66. Funny part is, I still feel much the same about cycling. How you ride is not a matter of age. What time has taught me is that the principles for traffic riding are true. They work. The governing factor or element of personal choice is how far you want to use and take them.

What I like about cycling — aside from being outdoors and the joy of movement — is that on a bike, you are naturally who you are. You can be timid and shy, or bold and brassy, and so long as you ride honestly and within your limitations, you'll be fine.

Trust yourself. Accept where you are at and plan accordingly. I have lived a life and pursued activities that some people would consider adventurous and risky. As a book editor, I have worked with people really functioning at the edge: record-depth deep sea divers, test pilots, astronauts, and similar.

All were skilled. And all were careful! They did not trust to the gods or take blind chances. They studied what they were doing and made sure they got it right. You can do the same, whether you are an innocent flower-child wafting along on the zephyrs of each day, or a world-wise warrior with nerves of steel in relentless pursuit of razor-clear goals.

I made a fuss about reading all of this book before buying a bike and setting off into traffic for the straightforward reason that you do have to plan ahead. It is a complete package: your attitude and how much you know about traffic riding; the kind of machine you use; and where you go.

The beauty is, it is under your control! If you can catch and believe and use this, you will be OK. You will actually have everything you need. Will there be mistakes? Sure, of course. Perhaps you have never used a map. You pick a route you think is good which turns out to be a nightmare of road works and steel plates and huge lumbering vehicles that threaten to squash you. So . . . get off and walk. Walking is fine. Walk happily for what you are!

Mistakes are for learning, and not all of them are fun. If you make a hash of lane-positioning and wind up stranded in the middle of a huge roundabout, you may well have a severe fright. Don't beat yourself up. Even very skilled riders and drivers make mistakes. This is exactly why people who are good always have a little in reserve, just in case. Control is comfort. If you regularly wind up in trouble and feeling uncomfortable, then you are exceeding your skill level. Back off. Start over.

You do not become a master by attacking, or through the sheer energy of your being. You become a master by learning to do things right. It takes time, and dedication, but . . . my favourite mantra — you can do it!

Details!

The general principles described in the previous chapter will help you sort out almost any situation. However, life is also in the details, and here are some you need to know about.

Cycle Path Hazards

Cycle paths which are completely independent of streets and roads are safe enough, and can be a wonderful treat. However, most urban cycle paths run alongside streets and hence are often very dangerous. The problem areas are intersections with other streets, and entrances and exits for driveways and parking areas. Motorists on the main street look out for traffic on the same street, but are typically unaware that they also need to check for two-way cycle traffic on a separate path. It is not just a problem of ignorance. Motorists may be unable to see cyclists approaching from behind on a separate path.

Another difficulty is that motorists about to enter or cross the main street stop directly athwart the cycle path. This is where they have to be in order to see if it is safe to go. Meanwhile, cyclists on the cycle path are blocked in both directions.

Black Spot, Camden, London

Motor vehicles turn right, across a two-way cycle path — a sure-thing killer. The volume of motor vehicle traffic is high, the set-up of the junction is strange, and drivers often go through without checking for cyclists coming from behind, or from around a blind corner in front.

A cyclist sensibly sticks to the safer main street.

Cycle Lane Divider

A variation on the parallel cycle path is a street divided by bollards and kerbs to form separate lanes for motor vehicles and cycles. This arrangement is a little better in that motorists can more easily see cyclists. A separate space can be a nice haven on a foul night or when motorists' behaviours become acutely base and mindless, as in rush hours. However, there is still the problem of motorists turning across or blocking your path at every side street, junction, and turning.

Cycle lane divider

Looks inviting, but at the horizon line, the cycle path abruptly ends. All traffic funnels into a single-lane, downhill bend — a formula for trouble. A cyclist, especially, wants to be in lane **before** such a situation.

Cycle Lanes

A cycle lane is a painted area on the road supposedly reserved for cycles. Do not be misled. As with cycle paths, cycle lanes can be highly dangerous. There is no problem on streets where painted lanes mark spaces which are logical courses for cyclists. However, some cycle lanes take idiotic paths; for example, close alongside parked cars, where a cyclist is at risk of being caught by an opening car door. Cycle lanes at high-traffic sites such as major roundabouts and bridges are often especially flawed. In some places, following a cycle lane is be a good way to get killed. I am sorry to be so trenchant, but just as bad roads cost lives, so do bad cycle lanes. My simple advice: always behave as what you are: a proper road vehicle. Ride the street. Ignore painted cycle lanes unless they fit in with your plans.

Idiot's Path

Would you like to meet a hard, unyielding car door? Follow the safety-marked cycle path!

Pedestrians

There are four cases: streets; shared-use paths; cycle paths; and pedestrian-only paths.

Streets and Roads

Careful! Pedestrians often do not 'see' cyclists and can waltz right into your path. A crash will hurt you both. Make allowances, even when you have the right of way. This will help avoid you becoming scared of a crash, and hence building up acrimony towards pedestrians. Remember the golden rules of flow and smoothness ... give a bit now and then, and you'll go faster and happier.

When a feckless pedestrian moves into your path, it can be dreadfully tempting to give a loud, angry yell, or deliberately ride close and brush their shirt-buttons to give them a fright. I understand! But . . just as slanging motorists only makes them dumber and meaner, going at pedestrians only promotes unfriendly vibes.

I whistle to give warning, or call 'Heads up!' if the situation is tight. Sometimes I quietly advise 'Look both ways' just as I pass behind someone who never knew I was there. Pedestrians are human beings. Treat them as you wish to be treated.

Shared-use

On shared-use paths slow down when pedestrians are about. They have right of way. Most such paths have an 8 MPH speed limit for cycles, with good reason. Pedestrians crossing a road know to check for vehicles, even if they often fail to do so. Pedestrians on a walking path are not expecting a cyclist to come whizzing around the next bend. The sudden appearance of a fast-moving bike is alarming, and even a bike moving at a sedate 5 to 8 MPH may cause concern.

Amiable coexistence with pedestrians: indicate you know they are there. Communicate. Tip a smile, a nod, a wink, or other courtesy, and make eye contact. Take note: if you approach people from behind, a bell or whistle may not work, because some people are deaf.

Cycle Paths

Pedestrians are cavalier about using cycle paths, especially in parks. Technically, you have the right of way, but don't make an issue of it. Give a little.

Pavements and Pedestrian-only Areas

Riding on pavements and in pedestrian areas is OK so long as you get off and walk when there are pedestrians about. From time to time newspapers run stories about the dreadful menace of pavement-riding cyclists. This is a cheap space-filler usually good for a rich crop of readers' letters. In fact, there are very, very few injuries from cyclist/pedestrian collisions. Ever.

Many times it is rational and sensible for cyclists to ride in a park or pedestrian area, rather than on a black-spot street known to be dangerous. Do it. Play by the rules and walk when pedestrians are about. If you are nabbed and get a ticket, take heart. The law is not always an ass. My daughter got a ticket for riding in a park on her way to school. The day before, she had been knocked off her bike by an opening car door, and was frightened of going on the road. In the park she had not been whizzing along, but rather, standing on one pedal and moving at a walking pace. I wrote the court and explained the circumstances, and the charge was dismissed.

Remember — when pedestrians are about, get off and walk. Pedestrians, little kids, and dogs deserve safe space, too.

Surface Hazards

Ye always scan ahead.

» Drains — Many have slots just the right size to snatch a bicycle wheel and fast-forward you to the Pearly Gates. I find it hard to believe how many thousands, perhaps even millions of these are around. They don't just lurk in the gutter, either; I saw a clever one just yesterday at a junction near Euston Station, positioned and angled perfectly in the path of cyclists pulling out of a side road. Said cyclists of course are looking to the side for motor vehicles . . .

» Metal plates, covers, lids . . . all tend to be slippery when wet.

» Wet leaves can be really slippery. This is obvious, of course, but it is surprising how often one can forget. Take a few leaves, mash with motor vehicle tyres until nicely pulped, add a sprinkle of rain, and presto! — down you go.

» New rain. Cars emit oils and other slippery substances, via exhaust haze and fluids dripping off vehicles. Drips are most evident in places where vehicles stop.

When there is a fresh rain, the water mixes with the oils and other fluids, and for a little while the road surface is slippery, sometimes acutely so. Once enough rain falls to wash the streets clean, traction improves.

So, be aware of the weather! If there has been a week without rain, and a light drizzle ensues, be very careful. Especially when stopping. Remember, it is not just you. The first bit of fresh rain is usually good for a rash of shunts and prangs by motorists.

» Gravel. Bikes skitter on gravel. It is generally not a big problem in cities, but you might encounter gravel or mud around construction sites.

» Glass. Watch for the glitter of broken glass. If you are forced to run through a patch, it is worth stopping and brushing your tyres clean with a rag or glove.

» Pot-holes. These things can be vicious. Slamming into a pot-hole is a shock, and can seriously damage a bike. If you are following behind a motor vehicle, you may not see a pot-hole until it is too late to avoid it.

Prevention is better than cure. On strange streets, ride with enough space up front to allow for hazards. If there is a prospect of trouble, shift your weight to the pedals, so the bike can rock back and forth underneath you.

If you are taken by surprise, do what you can. Stand on the pedals, press the bike down, then lift and rotate the bike up and forward, lifting with both arms and legs. This is a manoeuvre you should practise in your cycle playground area, using bits of foam or cloth to mark a 'pot-hole'.

Councils have a legal obligation to maintain roads properly. If you or your cycle are damaged as a result of hitting a pot-hole, you can claim against the council responsible.

» Bumps. A bump is reverse pot-hole and is handled the same way. Alas, while pot-holes are not supposed to be there, speed-control bumps have become a popular feature for urban streets. It is easy to understand why. Bumps force motor vehicles to 20 MPH and less and thereby save lives. 'Sleeping policemen' are a lot cheaper than human police, and are on the job 24/7.

Speed cushions, or pads, are no problem for cyclists. You just run in the space between the cushions. Speed bumps or platforms which run across the entire road are a nuisance. If you sit slack in the saddle, the impact is uncomfortable. You have simply got to master the stand-and-press routine.

With pedals even, raise up slightly then press down sharply

It is all in the timing. You need to press the bike down just as you come to the bump. It helps if you have big, slightly squishy tyres. But even with narrow, hard tyres, if you catch the right moment, the bike will lighten up while rocking over the bump.

» Rail and tram tracks. Meet these at an angle wide enough to ensure your wheel does not get caught, or pushed to one side. Simple technique, but in heavy traffic, veering enough for a good line of attack can be difficult. If there are tram lines or railway tracks around, plan your moves well in advance.

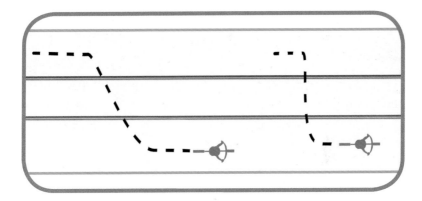

Cross tram lines at 45° at least. 90° is better!

» Grids. Metal grids are sometimes encountered on bridges. If the grid is made of small squares, it may form lines which can catch or destabilise a bike. The solution is to weave back and forth, so that you cross the lines at an angle, as for tram lines and railway tracks.

Motor Vehicles

» Turns. Motorists have mastered the secret of invisibility. For a left turn, they will pull alongside or just ahead of a cyclist, and make a left turn right across the path of the now-invisible cyclist. Watch for this, it happens all the time. Prevent by protecting your space. Ride centre-lane and do not allow a motor vehicle to overtake. If a vehicle proceeding ahead of you indicates a left turn, move to the right side of the lane, or into the next lane over, so you can more easily go around the turning vehicle without losing momentum. Lane-changing in heavy traffic may take muscle, and an easier alternative may be to touch the brakes and slow a little until the turning vehicle clears from your path.

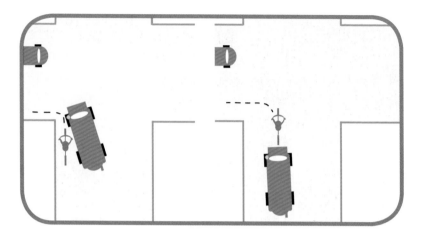

The left-side position allows motorists to overtake and cut in. Occupying the centre lane holds the motorist in place behind the cyclist.

» Big 'Uns. Have you ever driven a bus or big lorry? A van with a closed back? If so, you'll know how difficult it can be for the driver to see to all sides and behind the vehicle. Ya don't, ya never, never, never position yourself between the side of a bus or long HGV and a hard place! If the vehicle turns, the rear will follow a tighter arc than the front, and you can be caught and crushed against a fence or some other object, or pulled underneath the wheels of the vehicle. Many cyclists have died this way.

Exactly because the rear of a long vehicle follows a tighter arc than the front, a big vehicle will start a turn by swinging wide in the opposite direction of a turn. When stopped at a junction, a big 'un which intends to turn left will be positioned somewhat to the right. An uninitiated cyclist may see an inviting gap on the inside of the vehicle, just the right size for a bike. An experienced cyclist knows it is the worse possible place to be.

A Rock and a Hard Place

Never position between a large vehicle and a fence or wall. If the vehicle moves inward, there is no escape. Because of the fence, the green painted cycle lane is a crock. The cyclists should be in front of the bus.

The cyclists, perhaps sensing the danger, have sensibly taken an early green and moved ahead of the bus. I wish they were further away from the kerb, though.

» Cross-turns. You are rolling along at a smart pace on two-way street. At a junction ahead, a motorist from the opposite direction is waiting to make a (right) turn across your path. You are trailing behind a couple of cars. Question: will the motorist wait until the cars are past and then turn in front of you? Answer: yes indeed, sometimes they will! If you are lucky, you may able to chomp the brakes and avoid a collision. If you are unlucky, well . . .

As ever, prevention is the line to take. Make sure you are at maximum visibility. Stand up and grow bigger, like a puffing-up bird. This ages-old territorial signal works (sometimes) with bears, and (sometimes) with motorists. Move to the right of your lane. Look at the driver. Do they see you? If they are on a mobile phone or otherwise lost to the moment, be ready for trouble.

One way to go through junctions is by running in the wake of a larger vehicle. You tuck in close behind and ride through on their size. Buses are good for this. Remember, however, to stay visible. If you tuck in very tight, a cross-turning motorist may not know you are there, and if they are the impatient type, they may dart behind the vehicle you are following and catch you on the fly. One way to be visible is to weave in lane, and even pull out as if about to overtake the vehicle in front. This will have you pointing straight at the motorist waiting to turn and will usually get their attention.

» Motorists about to enter or cross a stream of traffic are a threat, because some of them do willy-nilly cut in front of cyclists. For prevention, ride on the high side, where you are most visible. This is right side of lane for a left-entering motorist, and left side for a motorist on the right. Try to catch the eye of the motorist. If they are not looking at you — watch out! Even if they do look at you, be on guard.

» Black-spots. Some places are more dangerous than others. Reasons why vary. Near my house there is a four-way junction with a traffic light. Motorists from all directions regularly run the lights, and I do not mean shade the amber. They blow through at speed well after the light is red! The risk is stupendous. The junction is not some lonely spot out in the boondocks, it is an intersection of two heavily trafficked main routes, with plenty of cross-turning vehicles. There have already been several nasty shunts, and there will be more.

Why motorists misbehave in certain locations is too evolved for discussion. Point is, I know about the junction, and I am always wary when using it. You, too, need to be familiar with your own territory. Indeed, one advantage of urban cycling is that through repeated local journeys, you gain a 'home ground' knowledge of the area around you.

» Car doors. Motorists enter and exit parked vehicles without regard for other road users. Stay far enough away from parked cars to be clear of an opening door.

You can watch for clues, such as seeing someone in a car, exhaust smoke, a face in a rear-view mirror, etc. You can still be taken by surprise (high seats/small people), and more important, you need to devote attention to other things. So, pure and simple, give parked cars a wide berth.

» Tailgating motorists. When unable to overtake, unskilled or immature motorists may crowd you, which of course is uncomfortable. Two things. One: to the extent that you can do so, plan ahead and try to avoid stacking up motorists behind you. This is when you need the broad overview of traffic as streams of motion. Two: do what you have to do.

» TFC motorists. Some motorists crowd too close alongside. They whiz by with an inch to spare, or pull up alongside and then move in on the cyclist.

As ever, ride position, and hold centre-lane. Cars coming up fast from behind is exactly when you do not want to edge to one side, as this invites motorists to squeeze by too close rather than pull out properly to overtake. Sometimes, when I know a motorist behind might be pushy, I deliberately wobble in an erratic fashion suggesting I cannot ride in a straight line, and might do nearly anything at any time.

Motorists who pull alongside and then edge sideways into your space are scary. You need a certain amount of side to side room in order to maintain control. If that space is compromised, you are endangered, and a typical reaction is to clutch the bars tight in an effort to maintain a straight line. This tension alone reduces control, often the result is a bail-out; slowing enough to put the motorist in front.

One cure is to take the initiative. When a motorist makes an untoward lateral move on you, turn the tables and move in on them. This gives you more space to play with, and is much safer than allowing the motorist to crowd you. How the script runs from here depends on a lot of things. Some motorists will become nervous and back off. Others will become aggressive. Still others may be unaware that anything is happening! You'll have to play the cards as they come, and of course, as you are able.

» Aggressive motorists. Motorists are aggressive by nature. Traffic involves conflicts over space which have to be resolved. Skilled and rational motorists know that firm behaviour and clear communication are the most effective techniques for resolving conflicts and lubricating the flow of traffic. They understand that working with others is the key to progress.

Incompetent and emotionally immature motorists think only of themselves and hence rely on aggression to resolve conflicts. As a result, they are often impeded and frustrated. When they encounter cyclists their behaviour can range from malicious harassment, such as passing too close, to outright attacks, such as cutting in and pushing a cyclist into the kerb.

What do you do? Stay alive! In any tight situation you will have your hands full simply maintaining control. Think guerilla, think escape, think live. Once clear, you will probably be very frightened, and possibly very angry. Do not let temper lead you into violent retribution, e.g. catching up the motorist and damaging their vehicle or person. You can be charged with menacing behaviour or assault. Physical violence is permissible only in self-defence. The motorist has to emerge from their metal cocoon and have a go at you. In self-defence you may put out their lights, so long as you use 'reasonable' force. If this is your bag, fine. It is not mine. Combat is mortal.

Short version: grin and bear it. I've spent time on the topic only because it is one for which feelings run high. It is hard to ride a bike without once in a while wanting to kill someone. But at the end of the day, you are not going to be able realign the minds and hearts of millions of motorists, nor single-handedly trounce them all. For a source of satisfaction which is productive, work on improving your own skills.

TAXI-CABS AND VANS

Driving a taxi-cab is one of the most stressful jobs in the UK. Professional cab drivers receive proper training and are usually OK on-road company, so long as communications are clear and sharp. Still, the skill of pro cabbies at vehicle handling means they often shave a little too close for comfort.

Mini-cab drivers are untrained, and can be a real problem. Many are upset from stress, and are routinely aggressive and intolerant. Mind they do not take you by surprise.

Drivers of commercial vans are also untrained, and often behave brutishly. Treat with caution.

» Killer Motorists. Sigh. Yes, it happens. There are people who will find a victim, and for fun, beat them to death. And there are people who use motor vehicles for homicidal attacks on cyclists and pedestrians.

Assault with a motor vehicle can be difficult to prove. Kill someone with a gun — even a robber intent on harming you — and you can go to prison or the funny farm for the rest of your life. Run down a cyclist with a car, and you may be let off with a fine and points on your license. The police, magistrates, and others involved in the criminal justice system, are prejudiced in favour of motorists over cyclists. I have lost track of the number of cases where motorists have deliberately attacked cyclists, and got away with it.

Which means? Honestly, I do not know. An answer might be as follows: worldwide, there are millions and millions of sharks. Yet in any given year, the number of shark attacks on humans is small, far and away fewer than would be the case if sharks were seriously intent on gobbling people. The situation with cars and killer motorists is pretty well the same. Any motorist has the potential for momentary rage and attack, but systematic assaults, though notorious, appear to be rare.

Ba-a-a-d People!

One problem with riding a bike is that someone can mug you for the bike. All-out assaults, as in being bombarded with bricks or clouted with a pole, do occur. More common is to be accosted by one or two tough-looking types, and told: 'We want your bike'. Does it happen in front of Harrods or Buckingham Palace? Not often, I expect. Does it happen in seedy neighbourhoods and on crime-ridden estates beloved of cycle path engineers and in general around the town? Yes, and fairly often.

If you know, I don't have to tell you. If you don't know, then please shed innocence. One of the great assets of cycling is that it puts you in the real world. You smell flowers and bakeries, you see pretty girls and boys, and you can meet muggers.

The basic tactic of mugging is intimidation. Experienced criminals can pick out likely victims by body language alone. They sense a person can be taken by surprise or is fearful, make a move, and if the victim rabbits as expected, go in for the snatch.

Defence starts with awareness. Keep your peepers going, especially when in rough areas. Give direct regard to anyone who might be a threat to you but do not stare in challenge. Muggers are looking for easy marks, not people who are aware and ready.

Riding the city is a bit like riding traffic. You have to appreciate where there may be sore spots or possible problems, and be guided accordingly. Some areas are OK by day, but not by night. Some places are just not OK! Learn your neighbourhood.

If you are accosted, stand firm. Co-operating with a mugger is never going to help. What if they wave a knife under your nose? Well . . . any idea of what a bicycle pump can do to an eye or throat?

The script for dealing with an outright attack on your person has to be yours. Keep in mind, attitude is important, but effectiveness at combat requires experience and a level of willingness to do harm which not all people possess. In most real life confrontations people say and do all sorts of funny things. It is both impossible and foolish to say what should happen. Do what is right for you.

Roadcraft

Big Doings

Multi-lane junctions and roundabouts are complex blends of fast-moving traffic streams. They require a positive approach, good positioning, and lane-changing at the right times. The start is the finish . . . meaning, how you ride one of these things depends on where you want to come out. A couple of examples:

» Two lanes turning left onto another street, also two lanes. The left-side lane carries on down the street. The right-side lane goes to a stop-line for a right turn onto a different street. If you are carrying on, you ride to the right of the left lane. If you are turning right, then you ride the centre of the right lane.

» Two-lane roundabout with four entrances and exits. From entry, for first exit left, ride the left lane; for second exit, the right lane; and for third exit, the right lane. Ride centre-lane. If you ride to the side or between lanes, vehicles will overtake on both sides.

The strategy is to minimise the number of times you cross traffic streams. If you ride a roundabout sticking on the left side (as some manuals mistakenly advise) you have to cross streams of incoming traffic. As well, you may be crossed by streams of outgoing traffic from the right (inside) lane. All this crossing and conflict substantially increases the risk of trouble. Changing lanes through a roundabout reduces the number of cross-flows. As well, carrying out positive, affirmative actions is a lot safer than staying in one lane and hoping for the best.

Inside Bends

Avoid being on the inside of motor vehicles through a turn. Turning vehicles (except those on rails) tend to follow a path which is a flatter arc than the actual radius of the turn, and to compensate, to clip or pass near the inside of the bend.

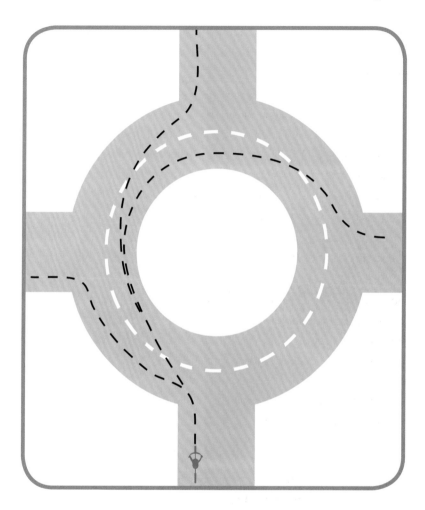

About a half mile from my house, there is a two-lane turn that is always a trouble spot. The turn is tight and hook-shaped. Even if I centre on the inside lane, cars from the outside lane still cut inside way too close. What I do now is centre on the outside lane, forcing all overtaking traffic to the inside.

This rider (circled) has done a good job of positioning in the correct lane for the left arm of a Y-split. For once, the location of the painted cycle lane makes sense.

You'll find similar problems wherever there are multi-lane turns onto fast streets.

High Side

There is a long queue of vehicles stopped for a traffic light. On the inside, between the vehicles and the pavement, the space is tight, and a rough road surface is sprinkled with broken glass and dog poops. On the outside, the road is clean and smooth with a clear run to the light — which way do you go?

If you do not have a reasonable idea of when the light will change, then neither! Overtaking should be done only with room and time to spare. You don't want to be passing on the outside and have the line of vehicles suddenly start moving. This noted, in most instances when traffic is queued, it is faster and safer to overtake on the outside than to filter through on the inside.

The high side, or centre of the road, is also the place to use for overtaking moving vehicles. Passing on the inside is bad policy. Motorists have difficulty seeing you, and in any case, are not expecting you to be there. If anything goes wrong, your space options may be very finite. Out on the high side, you are much more visible, the road surface is usually better, and your space options are wider.

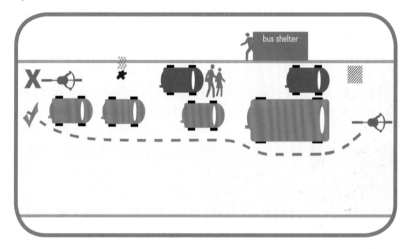

The space options on the inside are very limited. On the high side there is a lot of room – and space to duck into, if the oncoming traffic is large or in a hurry.

Riding the high side, you usually need to keep moving at a good rate. You'll be looking well ahead, planning in advance which breaks and openings to take. It is all quite engaging, and so it is important to remind you that you are not the only two-wheeler out there. The high side is active territory for other cyclists, scooters, mopeds, and big, powerful motorcycles. Do not be taken by surprise. Scooter and pizza delivery moped riders are often inexperienced and can be extremely reckless. Riders of big motorcycles are more seasoned, and are usually courteous toward cyclists, but nonetheless want to move along. Let them by at the first opportunity.

Rolling Stop

Fully stopping and then starting up a bike is a bit of a production. It is much easier to execute a rolling stop, braking and slowing to a point where you are motionless for a moment, then releasing the brakes and moving ahead. A rolling stop must be done with distance to spare between the stop-point and the street, junction, or whatever, you are entering. As well as your own safety, you need to consider other road users. Cut a stop too fine, and motorists already on the cross-street cannot know if you intend to stop. In fact, they are obliged to assume you will not, and may brake hard, or even panic-stop. Use a rolling stop only when there is clear space, with good sight-lines.

Traffic Signals

Your impulse should be to obey traffic signals. However, there are times when it is OK or even best to ignore lights.

In the Netherlands, it is common practice to green-light cyclists ahead of motorists. This allows the cyclists to be out of the way and moving in an orderly fashion when the motorists start off. If the groups start together, the differences in speeds causes conflicts and problems.

It is OK to 'advance green light' when the way is clear. Some situations are more feasible than others. A left turn at a T-junction from a one-way street hardly raises a ripple, provided there is no cross-traffic. Crossing a major multi-lane two-way road against the lights, however, may cause waves.

What about legality and the law? If you value the law above all else, then by all means act as is right for you. I go by what is best for traffic flow, and for me. For example, near my house, on a route I use often, there is a two-lane run-up to a T-junction left turn onto a single lane. Two into one on the turn produces a lot of conflict between motor vehicles. A smart cyclist takes an 'early green' and gets well clear of the problem area. This helps the motorists, too.

One type of traffic light has a pedestrian-only green period. If there are no pedestrians around, fine to go. When pedestrians are about, it depends on where they are moving, and who they are. If they are crossing your path, then no. If they look the sort to be upset, also no. If they are to one side, then perhaps.

Generally, do not run lights if there is cross-traffic, or if there are pedestrians who might be upset. The issue is not whether you can get away with it, because often you can. The point is that you should not unduly upset other road users.

Brethren

Competitiveness is a natural instinct, and the presence of other cyclists travelling in your direction may lead you to pedal harder. Street duels range from mild dicing on commuting runs with riders striving to be out front without evincing apparent effort, to wild, all-out races between fit riders who know how to handle traffic. Fast street riding can be fine fun, but guard against becoming over-zealous. It is easy for one thing to lead to another, and for riding to then crowd margins of safety, or standards of courteous behaviour to other cyclists. This is more of a problem with amateurs than with veterans, who usually know when to back off. In particular, do not

» Push through queues of cyclists stopped for a traffic signal.

» Draft (follow another cyclist closely) unless you both know exactly what you are doing, and the road is well clear.

» Overtake and then slow down. This is perhaps the most common amateur error and is a thorough nuisance for riders intent on maintaining a steady pace. After you overtake, keep going and stay clear.

» Conversely, when someone is overtaking you, do not suddenly pedal harder. Let them by.

» Overtake and, in the process, box a cyclist against an obstruction. Especially on commuting runs, riders sometimes overtake slowly. Fine on an open road, not so good in dense traffic. Overtake cleanly, without interfering with the other rider.

» Cut closely in front of another cyclist. It takes only a touch of a front wheel against the rear wheel of a bike ahead to send a rider down.

Competition is fun and healthy. On the track or on the street, ride clean. Look after your brethren.

CRASH DRILL

First, sort out if you are OK, or need help. Remember, shock and/or adrenaline can mask injuries.

For a solo crash caused by a road defect, make notes on physical specifics, such as size of a pot-hole, location of barrier without warning light, etc. A photo can be useful.

For a crash involving another vehicle, obtain names, addresses, and if relevant, driver licenses and vehicle registration numbers. Never admit fault. Any witnesses, ask for contact details.

Any crash which may involve a claim for personal injury or damage to the bike should be reported to the police. This is for insurance purposes. If the crash involved a motor vehicle and you believe the driver was at fault, do not expect the police to prosecute.

If you have taken a tumble, see a doctor at the earliest opportunity. You can be hurt without knowing it. If you are hurt, then as well as obtaining care, you need to establish that the harm was caused by the crash.

Insurance claims . . . oh boy. Go at an insurance company on your own, and you'll have a long, tough ride. My best advice: now, today, join a cycling group that will provide free legal help if you need it. Contact the Cycle Campaign Network, 54 - 57 Allison Street, Digbeth, Birmingham, B5 5TH (www.cyclenetwork. org.uk/groups/groups.html) for a group near you.

School

Richard Grant was riding an original Marin County clunker, the first in the UK. I was aboard a spanking new Specialised Stumpjumper mountain bike, one of the first produced in 1981. We were on a ridge in one of London's parks, poised above a slope that plunged steeply down for some 70 metres before levelling out in the forest below.

"Come on, Richard," said RG, "I'll show you what these bikes can do… follow me," whereupon he dropped off the edge and straight down the slope! I thought, 'If he can do it so can I,' chomped the brakes, and let it happen, sliding back out of the saddle as the bike tilted over the edge, then hanging over the rear wheel and feathering the rear brake as the bike slid and danced down the slope. Easy!

For the rest of that day we charged around the park, finding ever-steeper and longer slopes to negotiate. I took to it like a duck to water, because I am used to skiing on the steep. But if Richard had not led me over that first drop-off, I would never have tried it.

Riding on the wheel of an experienced cyclist can be a great way to learn. However, leading a novice cyclist through traffic requires a high level of skill. Hence, I was cheered when a couple of cycling friends told me that they were studying to become certified cycling instructors, but had failed the graduation exam on their first attempt. My friends are excellent cyclists. They were failed for not listening carefully enough to their students. Right on! Teaching is a professional skill. And thankfully, professional teaching of assertive cycling techniques is available in Britain.

The leading organisation training cycling instructors is Cycle Training UK (020 7582 3535 and www.cycletraining.co.uk). As well as offering courses for instructors, they provide one-on-one instruction for individuals, families, and groups, in the London area. Instructors will cycle any journey with a student, and rental bikes are available. Another good school offering private training at all levels is the London School of Cycling (020 7249 3779 and www.londonschoolofcycling.co.uk), run by Patrick Field. The LSC has been going since 1992 and also offers courses in bike maintenance.

Some people learn best or most quickly from other people, and if you are such a person, then private instruction will be richly worthwhile. Another option for instruction are cycle training courses run by councils. With the general impetus to promote cycling as transport, many councils are offering courses, often run by instructors who can also provide private tuition. Check with your local council and see what's going.

Finally, and certainly not least, many cycling groups run bike mate schemes. Under this plan, an experienced cyclist will join you for a ride to work, or other journey, and do what they can to show you how to make it all work. Mind, this is not professional tuition, but may still be very useful.

V: MECHANICS

Maintenance

How well a bike performs depends on how well it is looked after. Happily, caring for a bike is a natural part of riding. A bike is a mechanical extension of your body, and so it is pretty easy to sense when servicing is needed. A squealing or juddering brake, ragged gear shifting, strange noises, and so on, are signals that mechanical attention is required. Especially if you do some of your own work, problems tend to be caught and dealt with early on, before they develop into major issues. A well-maintained bike rarely suffers anything worse than a puncture.

Maintenance involves cleaning, lubrication, adjustment, and replacing parts. Cleaning is to keep away dirt, which is abrasive and causes wear. Lubrication is to help parts run smoothly and prevent rust. Adjustment is to keep components performing properly. Replacing parts is done when consumables such as brake shoes, tyres, and cables, or components such the chain or gear changers, have done their time.

Some people enjoy maintenance, others do not. If you are in the latter group, fine; have your bike regularly serviced by a shop, or a home-visit mechanic. Of course, even if you are a capable bike mechanic, some servicing jobs require specialised tools and skills, and are best done by a shop. First move for keeping a bike in shape is to line up one or two good shops for servicing work.

Picking a Shop

Bike shops vary from large, centrally-located emporiums filled with lots of bikes and staff, to modest-size neighbourhood shops with a few machines and a couple of staff. Regardless of size, some evidently concentrate on road racing bikes, downhill mountain bikes, or whatever; others are geared toward transport and utility bikes. There is an element of horses for courses; a racing bike is best off at a shop that specialises in such machines, while an ancient roadster may find more skilled ministrations in a shop that the years have passed by.

Bikefix Workshop, London

Literally a little laid back, Bikefix do a lot of work on recumbents and folders, as well as a wide range of utility cycles. In doorway: the Norwich Twitcher, a.k.a. cycle designer Mike Burrows.

The important thing is that you like and trust the shop. A location near home or work can be helpful. Ask cyclists in the area which shops they have used for repairs, and how they got on with them. Expect to hear a few complaints. Even the best shops pull boners once in a while. But if reports are mostly positive, that's a good start.

For objective criteria, cycle mechanic training and certification schemes are now well-established. Perhaps the best-known is CyTech, run by the Association of Cycle Traders. Many manufacturers also have training courses. All of this is good, because correct training and equipment is essential for servicing modern components. Especially if you have a high-tech machine with features such as disc brakes or suspension, a certificate or two on the shop wall is a plus.

Freelance Mechanics

More than a few enterprising souls have set themselves up in business as mobile bike mechanics. Some are independent, others are agencies. Services range from home or workplace visits for routine maintenance, to emergency call-out road repairs. Most are bike-based and work by regions. Can be very handy. Ask around, run a Google check, to find someone in your area. Ask a prospective mechanic what jobs they can do, and ask for and check references.

Dealing With Shops

The most basic rule is: all work, whether small or large, routine or extraordinary, should be covered in a written estimate, inclusive of cost and a completion date. If, while servicing your bike, the shop discovers that further work is needed at increased cost, they must check with you before proceeding. The exception is if, at the outset, you instruct the shop to do what needs doing. Stating the obvious, you should do this only if you know and trust the shop.

Condor Cycles Workshop, London

As befits a top shop producing lots of high-end, classy machines, the workshop is well-organised, pristine, and efficient.

Care is needed; some shops steal. One of my daughters was ripped off by a south London shop which charged £40, labour only, to change a tyre! Grrrrr! She hadn't imagined so simple a job required an estimate. To support the ransom demand, the shop made up fairy tales about what they had done. Never leave yourself open to this kind of abuse. Responsible shops provide an estimate; if one is not forthcoming, go elsewhere.

Shop Jobs

An estimate is also for the protection of the shop. If you believe work on bikes should be cheap, lose the idea! A decent bike check and run through basic adjustments and lubrication will see little change if any from £50. If replacement parts are involved, the bill can easily push £100.

Some shops offer package tune-up and servicing deals. Stage one might be a mechanical check, adjust brakes and gears, lubricate chain, check/ adjust bearings, and true wheels. More extensive might be above, inclusive of replacing worn parts as necessary, plus clean and repack bearings throughout. Package deals are economic because the bike is simply done, without back-and-forth palaver about whether or not a particular job is strictly necessary. Watch your step on replacing worn parts, as while labour is included, parts are extra. If a bike needs this level of service, better to have a survey and specific estimate.

If you book ahead, a shop near your place of work can do same-day service; drop off in the morning, ride home in the evening.

Check!

When you collect a bike from a shop, always check that all work has been done correctly. Bike mechanics, too, occasionally burn the toast. Spin the wheels, test the gears and brakes, and do all the things you would do if meeting your bike for the first time.

Doing For Yourself

A Book of the Words

You need a maintenance manual. Once, bikes were mechanically of a muchness, and a manual could be comprehensive. Modern cycle technology includes a wide range of designs and innovations. Setting down servicing instructions for everything available would require a hugely thick volume — and before the ink was dry, such a tome would be outdated by changes and new designs.

In any case, organising an up-to-date maintenance manual that is specific to your bike is easy, and free. All you need is a computer with Internet access. A bike consists of frame and components. Bike manufacturers (the brand name on the frame) are slow on providing on-line maintenance information. However, component manufacturers are usually exactly opposite! Find the manufacturer(s) of your components, and you can access and print servicing instructions in detail — voila, a custom maintenance manual for your bike.

Of course, to service a bike you need to know something about mechanical work. This book covers some basics; for more, the Internet again positively bursts with information — a Google check for 'bike maintenance' produced over two million hits. As you might guess, bike tool makers are happy to explain how to use their stuff; a fine example is www.parktool. com/repair/. There are also web sites with free information on servicing by bike-tech saints such as Jim Langley (http://www.jimlangley.net/wrench/ wrench.html) and Captain Sheldon Brown (http://www.sheldonbrown. com/repair/index.html). These people are especially good, because they have both a lot of practical experience with professional bike maintenance, and really enjoy communicating. You get warm encouragement, and those kind of inside tips that make jobs easier and better. Another good share fun and information site: http://www.utahmountainbiking.com/index.htm. Includes how to print out instructions.

Many councils and cycle groups offer cycle maintenance courses. Many are free, or low-cost. Try Ride Manchester (ridemanchester.org.uk) and Transport for London (tfl.gov.uk/cycles/maintenance).

In this book, we'll cover the high ground, roughly equivalent to the 'Quick Start' information sheets supplied with computers and cameras, but (I hope) a little better. I'll dip into a few replacement of components jobs, but as said, there is not the space to do them all.

NB: for information on adjusting components for fit, for example the reach of a brake lever, see the chapter on Fitting A Bike, p.112.

Tools

Most maintenance can be done with a few tools. Use good-quality tools that work well. Cheap tools are frustrating to use and can damage a bike. The tools you need depend on the type of bike and how it is built, and on how far you are going with maintenance.

Basic

» Air pump (details under Tyres, below).

» Tyre levers.

» Cross-head and flat-blade screwdrivers, small (but not tiny).

» Allen (hex) keys — 2 to 6 or 8 or even 10 mm.

All-in-one-tools with screwdrivers and hex keys are compact and handy for carrying on a bike. However, separate tools are easier to use. For hex keys, best are the type that are rounded at one end. This makes it much easier to engage a bolt and/or work at off-angles when space is cramped.

» Spanners — 8, 9, and 10 mm are the most common sizes.

» Spoke key — used to adjust spoke tension.

Rounded-end hex key

Depends on Your Bike/Level of Servicing

» Adjustable spanner — 15- or 20-cm length. Useful for bolt-on wheels.

» Wire cutter — Essential for neatly cutting cable wires and cable housings. Ordinary pliers won't do!

» Small metal file.

» Hub cone spanners — Flat, thin spanners for hubs with adjustable bearings.

» Headset spanners — Extra-large spanners for adjusting headset. Sizes vary. Not needed for threadless headsets.

» Socket spanner, 15 mm — For older bikes with bolt-on cranks.

And

A cycle work stand. This holds a bike up in the air for easy access, allows spinning of transmission and wheels, and makes adjusting brakes and gears lots easier and more fun. The problem is cost, and if money matters, one solution is to share with friends. A half-dozen people or more can easily use the same stand.

Absent a work stand, it is often possible to jury-rig ropes to lift a bike into the air. Or if you are handy with wood, to construct a stand or other means of holding the bike. The super no-frills option is simply to turn the bike upside-down, on

saddle and handlebars. To avoid scratching the bike or mashing cables, use a cardboard box with slots cut for the handlebars, and place a pad under the saddle. Take it from me. If you're going to run bikes seriously, then buying or making a proper work stand is a good investment.

NUTS AND BOLTS

Nuts and bolts and many parts fit together via spiral grooves called threads. When initiating assembly, it is important to align the threads correctly, else the parts not go together, or cross-thread and have a weak connection. To get a feel for correct threading, practise with a nut and bolt. Put the two together, and reverse (anti-clockwise) the nut or bolt, until the land (raised portion of thread) on one settles into the valley (groove portion of thread) of the other. There will be a distinct tactile click. Then slowly turn in (clockwise) the bolt/nut until the parts are fully engaged. None of this is rocket science, it is the same thing you do when screwing a top onto a bottle. However, bike parts have much finer threads; hence the need to refine your touch.

When tightening nuts and bolts, be firm but not brutal. Many bike parts are made of aluminium alloy and over-tightening can strip threads. Use lock nuts when possible. These have a plastic insert that prevents the nut from slipping, but allows it to be tightened or undone. Another tactic is to use a securing substance such as Loctite. This works best after a bike has been used a bit and the parts have bedded in and been tightened.

Use alloy or stainless steel bolts. Ordinary steel bolts quickly rust.

NB: the left side (as you face in same direction as bike) pedal has a left-hand thread and is undone clockwise.

A Word

When disassembling parts, be methodical and tidy. Note how things go together. That washer, is it flat or curved? If the latter, which way does the curve go? If need be, make notes. Keep bits and pieces in containers. Old jars, tins, or egg cartons will do.

Tyres

The single most useful performance aid for a bike is an air pump! Tyres are your contact point with the ground, and strongly affect your comfort, safety, and efficiency. You want the right air pressure for your tyres, weight, and riding conditions. A variation of as little as 5-10 psi (pounds per square inch) can make a difference. Tyre pressure should be checked and topped up, once a week.

Pump

A good-quality small hand pump that you can carry easily is essential in case of a puncture. Super-short models take an age to work, and may only produce weak pressure. Good-quality compact models, however, can work a treat. I'm fond of my Blackburn MDS-1 Mommoth.

I'm fonder still of a full-size track (floor) pump, the kind you set on the floor, hold with a foot, and pump with both hands on the handle. These fill tyres fast, and have a built-in pressure gauge. If you use bikes a lot, a track pump is an asset worth having. One can easily be shared between several cyclists. Another route is to find a cycle shop that provides track pumps for customers' use.

Never use a petrol station air line to fill a bike tyre. The volume of air in a bike tyre is small, and it takes but seconds to over-inflate and blow tyre and tube to smithereens with a huge bang.

How Much Puff?

Look at the tyre side wall; it will state a pressure range in psi or bar. The right pressure for you depends on several factors. One is weight; if you are heavy, go toward the top of the range. Another is what you want: for speed, go harder; for a bit of comfort, go softer. In slippery conditions, a softer tyre may have a little more grip. Careful, though; a softer tyre is more vulnerable to damage from sharp impacts.

This one is max. 7.0 BAR or 100 psi

Pumping!

Remove valve cap. There are three types of air valves: Schrader, Presta, and Woods.

Valves: from left, Woods, Presta and Schrader

A Schrader valve has a spring-loaded pin inside the stem. The pin has to be depressed in order for air to flow in or out. Hence, a pump with a Schrader fitting (the business that goes onto the stem) has a stub in the centre to press down the spring-loaded pin. Often there is a lever that both moves the stub and grips the valve stem. (A few special-design pumps have a rotating mechanism that does the same thing.) Place fitting over the valve, press down, and trip the lever. It may take a couple of tries before you get a good fit. If the fitting is straight off the barrel of the pump (no hose), take care when pumping to hold the pump steady, and not yank the valve stem. When done, undo lever and remove pump. Replace cap; it helps keep out grit.

A Presta valve is a proper piece of kit that can take high pressures. Undo the little knurled knob at the end of the stem. The pump fitting must be for a Presta valve, and is a pressure fit. Place fitting directly over valve and push down until the valve is firmly gripped. Don't wiggle! If the valve does not have a holding ring and sinks down, use your fingers to brace it from behind.

Pumps for Presta valves have a ring around the rubber washer that engages the valve stem. Tighten this if the connection is loose.

Pump, and again, if you are using a pump without a hose, take care not to jerk the valve about, or else the little knurled bit may get bent. For the same reason, when you are done, do not wiggle the pump to and fro to get it off. Instead, give it one sharp, direct blow with the hand to knock it free.

A Woods valve is an antique, and has its own design fitting for connecting a pump. Happily, a Presta pump also works fine. Push fitting down over stem and pump.

Tyre Care

An ounce of prevention is worth a pound of cure. Avoid brutal impacts (ruptures) by actively helping your bike through pot-holes and over obstacles, and cultivate an eye for sharp road litter (cuts). If you unavoidably run through some glass, pull over and take a moment to brush the tyres clean with a rag or glove.

When you do regular maintenance, check the tyres for embedded particles, cuts, and bruises. Replace tyres sooner rather than later. If cost makes you flinch, keep in mind: wheels are dynamic and tyres especially so; quality tyres enhance every moment of riding.

Cleaning

Dirt is the enemy! A working bike needs a wash every two weeks or so, depending on conditions. Mild soap and water and a pail or bucket will do. Biodegradable detergents are OK, fierce detergents may harm a waxed or polished finish. A sponge or rag is good for surfaces, a brush is handy for nooks and crannies. If you have rim (calliper) brakes, make sure you clean the rims. Water is OK for disc brakes. Avoid washing or rinsing too vigorously around bearing seals (hubs, bottom bracket, headset). Wipe bike dry.

Back when, after a muddy day in the Welsh hills, we would pay local kids 50 pence to clean our bikes by riding them in the river. The kids had a ball. We had to re-lubricate thoroughly right away, though. This is the score with other instant-action techniques such as using a high-pressure spray or sticking a bike in the shower. It is easier to clean lightly and often.

For really dirty machines, bike shops sell special cleaners that churn dirt and other contaminants into a froth that will rinse off with water. They work pretty good. Bike shops also sell solvents for cleaning greasy parts such as the transmission. Petrol works well but is genuinely dangerous; the volatile vapour is heavier than air, and can pool and creep

Keep that badge shined bright and it will help the bike to fly!

along the ground. If it meets a flame or spark — whumpf! Paraffin is less combustible, but contains water. Parts have to be carefully dried. If you want a whiz solvent, get something from a bike shop that will work without adverse consequences. Alert: use only water for disc brakes; degreasing and cleaning agents may contaminate the disc rotor or pads. If this happens, clean ASAP with isopropyl alcohol (safe) or acetone (hazardous!).

Polish will help keep a bike clean and shining. What to use can vary from easy-use household furniture polishes to rub-rub-rub auto paste waxes. A middle road is a silicone polish. Your fancy. Whatever, if you have rim brakes, do not wax or polish the wheel rims!

Lubrication

Bikes use lubricant in two forms: liquid and grease. Liquid is for light use — pivot bolts, chain, cables, and similar — and grease is for bearings and coating parts to prevent corrosion.

Home-brew concoctions aside, there are two types of lubricants: petroleum-based or synthetic. Use one or the other, as they are sometimes incompatible. If the wrong types meet, the result can be a fight, and a sticky mess that is anything but slippery.

Petroleum-based oils and greases are cheap, and effective so long as they remain clean. Alas, they attract dirt, and have poor resistance to water and are easily washed away. Far superior are modern synthetic lubricants, which in liquid form divide into two broad groups: dry and wet. Dry lubricants tend to be waxy and clean and less durable, and are more often used in summer and dry, dusty conditions. Wet lubricants tend to be oily and more durable, and are more often used in winter and wet conditions. Wet or dry, some liquid lubricants are available in both light- and heavy-duty versions, for use as required in fair or adverse conditions.

TIPS

Cultivate a good supply of rags. Best are old towels, worst are hardsynthetics.Develop the habit of wiping your bike down after a wet ride. It will help prevent tarnishing and extend the interval between proper washes. If you take a winter ride and the roads have been salted, wash the bike thoroughly ASAP. Salt does horrible things to aluminium alloys.

Some lubricants are available in both liquid and grease form. This is good, because it ensures compatibility if you refresh a greased component with a little liquid lubricant. As for which . . . some are better (or worse) than others, and most mechanics have favourites. I like Pedros Syn-Lube, and also use Finish Line and Lightning with complete success. Any well-known brand is likely to be fine. The keys to success with lubrication are regular and correct application, and not using too much. Excess attracts dirt, and forms an abrasive compound — exactly what is not wanted.

Older bikes may have adjustable bearings that require servicing and lubrication with grease. Most modern bikes use sealed bearings for components such as hubs, headset, and bottom bracket. You do not have to lubricate these.

You do have to look after the chain (unless it is fully enclosed), the gear changer(s), freewheel, brake mechanisms, exposed controls such as brake levers, and cables.

Regular lubrication is required for the chain, the gear changer(s), freewheel, brake mechanisms, exposed controls such as brake levers, and cables.

Chain

In Ye Olden Days, bike chains were regularly cleaned and lubricated, a process that involved removing the chain from the bike and putting it through a sequence of cleaning and lubricating processes. With modern lubricants, a chain can stay on the bike, and simply be lubricated and wiped clean.

Petroleum-based oil is cheap and works great, but only if the chain is fully enclosed. On an open chain, it attracts dirt, which necessitates frequent, thorough cleaning — you don't want to know. Synthetic lubricants are better because they are cleaner.

Application: place a little lubricant on every link. If you are in a hurry, an aerosol delivers quickly, but at risk of excess. I prefer a simple squeeze bottle. Hold so the nozzle just touches the chain, and use the cranks to slowly rotate the chain while lightly squeezing the bottle to deliver a little lubricant to each roller. Less than a drop will do; just get it wet. When the whole chain is done, spin the cranks and run the chain around for a while to work the lubricant in. Then wipe the chain clean, by holding a rag around it while spinning the cranks. Wipe, and wipe again; the important place for the lubricant is inside the rollers and pins. Wipe the chain again a day or two later, after riding has pushed out more lubricant and dirt.

A clean, lubricated chain is not for show. A dirty chain is inefficient, wears quickly, and increases wear on the chain rings and freewheel sprockets. Replacing all this lot costs a packet!

Clean the chain ring(s) and, if you have a derailleur system, the tension and jockey rollers (see below), when you do the chain.

Gear Changers

Derailleurs

Check the tension and jockey rollers for caked dirt; clean with a screwdriver or rag. Give both rollers a shot of lubricant, and work in. Lightly lubricate the pivot points of the derailleur, work the derailleur around to help the lubricant penetrate, then wipe clean.

pivots

pivots

rollers

Hub Gears

Follow manufacturer's instructions. There are several makes of hub gears in use, and types and quantities of lubricants required vary. Internal hub gears are complex mazes of minute parts, and using the wrong stuff can gum up the works.

Freewheel

The inside of the freewheel needs a shot of lubricant every month or so. Lay the bike on its side, freewheel up, place a little lubricant on the join line where the outer part of the freewheel rotates around the inside part, and spin the wheel to work the lubricant inside the freewheel body. Wipe away any excess.

Brake Levers

Brake levers like a touch of lubricant on the pivot bolts.

Brake Mechanisms

Hub brakes need a little grease on the pivot pins for the arms, every year or so. Although dismantling a hub brake is usually not rocket science, this job is perhaps best left to a shop.

Disc brakes should be serviced strictly according to manufacturer's instructions. You absolutely do not want to get anything slippery on the rotor disc, or pads.

Cantilever and V-brakes with arms that rotate on studs called bosses are the common type, and need a small amount of lubricant on the bosses. Ideally, these are greased; release spring tension on the brake mechanism (see overleaf), undo the pivot bolts, remove the arms (carefully noting the position of any springs or other bits), clean everything thoroughly, grease the bosses (outside only), and re-mount the arms.

It is good practice to fix the pivot bolts in place with an anti-slip substance such as Loctite. Naturally, you want this stuff only inside the boss where the pivot bolt engages, and not on the outside of the boss where the brake arm rotates! Cleaning and lubricating brake arm bosses is a straightforward job, but it does require the right tools and materials, and neat execution. If there is not time nor means for disassembly, a small amount of liquid lubricant where the brake arm rotates on the boss can be helpful. Not too much or it will seep down to the brake shoes.

Clean and grease pivot bolts

1. Pull back cover

2. Noodle is exposed

3. Lift off noodle

4. Unscrew pivot bolt

5. Remove brake arm

6. Note where pin fits into boss -see picture 7

7. Boss

8. Apply grease

9. Apply Loctite…

10. …Inside only!

11. Replace brake arm

12. Replace pivot bolt

13. Replace noodle

Brake arm bosses should be greased, oh, twice a year.

Quality calliper brakes are self-contained; they include their own pivot bolt(s). Designs vary, but the basic principle is still for the arms to rotate on bolts that should be kept clean and lubricated. Ensure that springs are disconnected before undoing the pivot bolts.

Cables

Lubricating cables can be tricky, because some modern cable housings and/or wires are coated with Teflon to reduce friction. Adding an incompatible lubricant can result in a sticky mess. On the other hand, if you have unlined cable housings or bare wires, then lubricating the wire and housing will make a real difference to performance. Which do you have? Ask at a bike shop.

For cables that should be lubricated, the usual procedure is to remove the cable wire from the housing, grease it, and reinstall it. See p. 256 on cables and wires for instructions. If you don't want to disassemble the cable wire and housing, it can be helpful to place a little liquid lubricant on the wire, near the housing. Arrange the parts so that gravity helps draw the lubricant inside the housing, and wiggle things about to help the lubricant work in. Wipe away any excess.

Brakes

One type of hub (drum) brake is operated by back-pedalling. Otherwise, brakes are operated by a lever on the handlebar, via a cable wire or hydraulic fluid. With use, a cable wire stretches, and hydraulic fluid evaporates or leaks out. As well, the pads used to generate friction (braking) abrade. These changes create slack in the system and increase the distance the brake lever must travel before the brake engages. In simple terms, there are three stages for dealing with this: adjustment; re-set system; and replace pads.

Hub brake

V-brake

Disc brake

Dual action calliper brake

Adjustment

Cable wire

Cable wire brakes have an adjusting barrel mounted either on the brake arm housing on the handlebar, or on the brake mechanism, or (rarely) midway on the cable. The barrel is held in place with a lock ring. Usually, both barrel and ring are knurled, so they can be turned with the fingers.

lock ring

barrel adjuster

It is OK to have the system set so that the brake lever is fairly close to the handlebar when the brake engages fully, as this gives small hands a more secure grip and enables faster response. However, there must be enough space between lever and handlebar for a clear margin of safety. When brake pad wear and/or wire stretch increases lever travel past this point, tighten up the system by undoing the lock ring (anti-clockwise), turning the barrel adjuster outward (anti-clockwise) a turn or two, and fixing it in place with the lock ring (clockwise). Is easy, you can do on the fly while riding, or waiting at a stop light.

Hydraulic

Hydraulic adjusting screw

Hydraulic brakes work by pushing fluid through a tube. To take slack out of the system, space for the fluid is reduced. How this is done varies. Some models have a knurled knob that is clear and proud on the brake lever mount; other models use a screw on the brake lever mount that sometimes is small and/or requires a specific tool. Either way, operation is dead simple: turn the knob or screw in (clockwise) until the brake lever travel is right.

Reset System

Once the adjusting screw, knob, or whatever, reaches the limit of travel, it is time to reset the system. This job involves tools.

Cable Wire

Undo barrel adjuster lock ring, turn barrel adjuster fully home (usually clockwise), and for wiggle room (more anon) reverse back out 1 or 2 turns. Next, disconnect or cancel the brake arm springs. How this is done varies by type of brake. With a calliper brake, you need to clamp the arms together, and it is worth having a simple, inexpensive tool called a third hand for this job. Arms can also be tied with tape or string, or held by your good friend Frodo.

Third hand tool

With cantilever brakes, disconnect the yoke cable. For V-brakes, slide back the rubber boot, and disconnect noodle from arm (overleaf). With a cable disc brake, disconnect the cable housing from the stop, or if a lever is used, tie the lever in place. Use the same technique for a hub brake.

Lifting the noodle to disconnect brake arm

The wire end is held by a cable anchor bolt. The wire may go around the side of the bolt and nest in a groove under a curved washer, or pass through a hole in the bolt.

Loosen the bolt (10 mm spanner, usually) just enough to pull the wire through (pliers may be handy), and tighten the anchor bolt. Tell Frodo to let go, or put the system back together (use the extra 1 or 2 turns in the barrel adjuster, if necessary), and test. You may have to go back to the well one or two times. With V-brakes, do not put the arms too close together, else they bump into each other.

Hydraulic

You must have the manufacturer's instructions. Basically, what must be done is to slack off the adjusting knob or screw, then add fluid to the system while bleeding air out of it. The type of fluid used, and how and where it is added, varies from model to model. The job must be done correctly, else braking power be lost, or the system damaged. As well, brake fluid can strip paint, ruin brake pads, and chew through some kinds of floors! You don't want any slip-ups. Either have comprehensive instructions and an ability to work very carefully, or take the job to a shop.

Adjust Pads

Rim Brakes

Adjusting rim brake pads is a seemingly simple job that can be frustratingly tricky to get right. The pad must strike the rim exactly so, the position of the pad is adjusted via bevelled washers, and the process can and usually does take repeated tries, because several dimensions are involved.

Pads must strike rim centre. Too high can abrade tyre — bad news — and too low can result in the brake arm diving under the rim and into the spokes, which is truly bad news. Set height first.

Pad must strike flat (but see below), and arc of travel must be through centre of rim. Otherwise, as the pad wears, the point of impact may shift too high or low. This is more of a problem with old-fashioned cantilever brakes, and less so with V-brakes and good-quality calliper brakes.

Leading edge of pad must contact rim a little before the rear edge. This compensates for play in the pivot bolts; when braking, the pad is fully against the rim. Otherwise, when braking, the pad can lift away from the rim. The classic symptom of this is loud squealing when the brakes are applied.

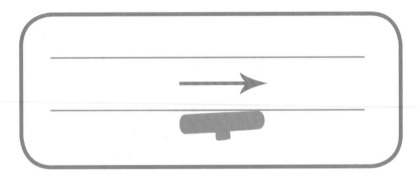

Toe-in. Arrow shows direction of wheel rotation

The amount of toe-in required varies according to the type of brake, and length of pad. With V-brakes, very little toe-in is needed, and some manufacturers say to use none at all. However, if the brakes squeal, try a small amount of toe-in; raise the back of the pad by the thickness of a calling card. Cantilever brakes need more, and cheap side-pull brakes with long arms may need a lot.

Do not be discouraged if it takes a while to get everything right. Persevere.

When the pads are properly aligned, apply and release the brake and check that neither pad drags on the rim. If so, centre the brake mechanism. In most cases, each brake arm will have a screw for adjusting the spring tension of the brake arm. Fiddle with the screws until the mechanism is evenly balanced.

Disc Brakes

You need manufacturer's instructions. In some cases, pads are self-adjusting.

Replace Pads

Brake pads can last hundreds or even thousands of miles, or be worn to nothing after one hard, muddy race. Dirt is abrasive, and keeping your wheels and brakes clean will prolong the life of pads. Periodically inspect the pad surfaces. Well before pads are fully worn, they will load up with grit and aluminium particles from the rim. Glazing weakens brake performance, and embedded particles will chew at the rim. Pads can be cleaned and renewed with a file or sandpaper, but eventually, the best course is to fit new pads.

Rim Brakes

Most rim brake pads include the mounting stud. One type is threaded, the other is not; make sure you get the right kind. When you remove the old stud/pad, carefully note the position of every washer and part. Replicate when you install the new pad, and then proceed as for as Adjusting, above.

One type of V-brake has a replaceable shoe. A tiny pin has to be removed, the old pad slides out, and the new pad slides in. Sounds easy, but isn't always. Follow manufacturer's instructions.

Disc Brakes

Absolutely a case of manufacturer's instructions! Again, keep a weather eye on disc brake pads, as in certain conditions they can wear rapidly.

Replace Brake Wire

Have the right wire for your brake. In particular, ensure that the nipple on one end of the wire is the design that fits your brake lever, and that length is sufficient; a long rear wire can be cut down for the front brake, but a short front wire will not reach the rear. Easy check: when purchasing wires, take your bike or the old wires to the shop.

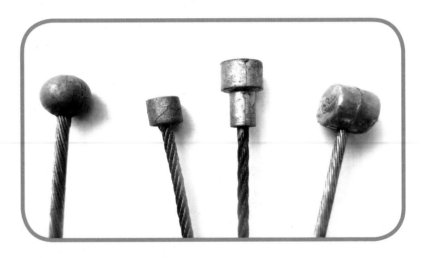

Wire ends

Double-check that the cable housings are OK. They should have no obvious kinks or problems. Any doubt, replace them, too.

You need a proper wire cutter (bike shops), a spanner for the cable anchor bolt (usually 10 mm), grease, and if you are doing the housing(s) as well, a file. You'll also need a means for preventing cut wire from unravelling — a metal clamp sleeve, tape, shrink-wrap, or glue.

Read the section above on adjusting brakes, it will explain some of the terms and moves referred to here. Relieve spring tension on the wire by disconnecting the brake mechanism or clamping the brake arms. A hub brake may not have this facility, in which case note where the arm is located. (You might be able to hold the operating lever in place with string or elastic cord.) Turn home the barrel adjuster and reverse out 2 turns. Undo the cable anchor bolt.

If you need to thread the wire out through cable housing(s), use the cutter to trim the wire end to a clean cut. When you thread out the wire, keep track of where the various cable housings, ferrules (cable housing caps), and other bits and pieces go. There is a purpose to each one.

If you are doing the cable housings as well, and need to cut the new ones to size, be sure to fit the cutter between the coils, else the cable end be mashed flat. Smooth off the end with a file.

Review section on lubrication. If appropriate, lightly grease the wire. Starting on the brake lever side, thread the wire through the housing. In most cases, the connection to the brake lever is via a slot. If so, do not connect yet; thread wire through cable housings, ferrules, cable stops, and what-else through to the cable anchor bolt. If the wire hangs up, turn it, taking care to rotate in the direction that wraps the wire strands, rather than opens them. Once through, connect nipple to brake lever, then seat cable ends into stops and ferrules. Lightly connect the anchor bolt. Go back over the system and make sure everything is snugly fitted together. It is common, for example, for a housing to snag on the lip of the barrel adjuster, or some other part. When all slack is removed, tighten the anchor bolt, and squeeze the brake lever hard several times. The wire may stretch a little. Re-set the anchor bolt and secure firmly. Trim excess wire with the cutter and prevent the end from unravelling by dipping in glue, wrapping with tape, clamping, or shrink-wrapping. Ya done it!

Gear Shifters

Adjustment

Hub

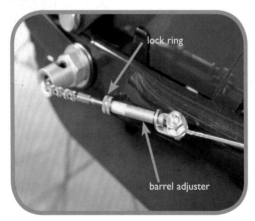

lock ring

barrel adjuster

Adjusting procedures for hub gears vary according to type and make. Especially if you have a fancier multi-speed system, it is worth having the manufacturer's servicing instructions. However, most hub gear systems have a barrel adjuster and lock ring for tuning the shift cable, located on the shift lever housing, or near where the cable connects to the hub. If your gears are missing shifts or skipping, then undo the lock ring (anti-clockwise) and give the barrel adjuster a half-turn or so (clockwise).

Try the gears. Possibly, you'll need to turn the screw some more, or even go the other way (anti-clockwise). Whatever, work a half-turn at a time, then test. The method is hit or miss, but will work.

Derailleur

Derailleur systems nearly always have a barrel adjuster on the shift control mount. Occasionally, there is a second barrel adjuster where the cable connects to the derailleur mechanism.

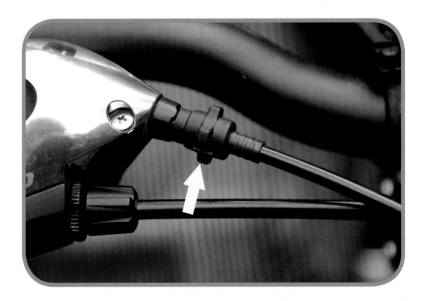

Barrel adjuster, handlebar

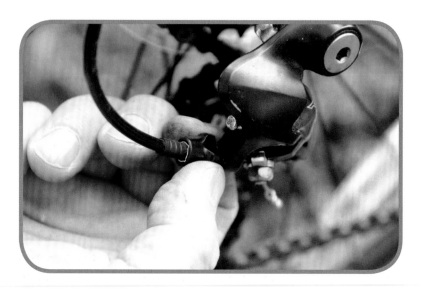

Barrel adjuster, derailleur

Unless you have an antique bike, the shift control(s) will be indexed; each shift moves the cable a set distance. In turn, the derailleur moves, pushing or dropping the chain from one cog or chain ring to another. When slack develops in the cable, shifts will miss or fail. To adjust, undo lock ring (anti-clockwise), turn barrel adjuster a quarter-turn (anti-clockwise), and test. Turn just a little at a time, as the adjustment is sensitive. Soon enough, you'll develop a feel for when the setting is on target.

If your shifter has gone way out of synch, shift to the small cog (rear) or small chain ring (front). Move the shift control one click and rotate the cranks. The chain should shift one cog or ring. If not, tighten barrel adjuster until it does. Check performance on all other cogs or rings. Sometimes, shifts are OK on one cog and not so hot on another . . . you may need to fiddle a bit to find a balance.

Re-Set System

When the barrel adjuster reaches the limit of travel, the system has to be re-set. Turn barrel adjuster(s) fully home, reverse 2 turns. Shift to smallest cog or chain ring. Loosen cable anchor bolt and pull wire through until it is snug. Tighten cable anchor bolt, and proceed as for Adjustment, above.

Replace Wire Cable

This is a job you can do yourself — but perhaps should leave to a shop. Two problems. First: There are many different kinds of shift controls, and nothing like enough space here to show them all. Some are simple, others have lots of parts. For how-to info, hit the Internet and download the manufacturer's instructions. Second: to minimise stretching, indexed systems use special wires and cable housings. These need specific tools for cutting. Best if a shop does this for you.

Assuming you have all the bits, run the chain to the small cog (rear) or small ring (front). Undo cable anchor bolt and thread out cable wire, taking careful note of the location and position of ferrules and cable housings. If appropriate, lightly grease the new wire, and starting with the shift control, thread the wire through the system, replacing ferrules and sections of cable housing as you go. Lightly fix wire end to cable anchor bolt. Check that all slack is out of system, then secure anchor bolt. Proceed as for Adjustment, above.

Derailleur, Rear Angle

The derailleur (or mech) must be free to move across the cogs. If it hits a cog (usually the biggest), loosen the mounting bolt and adjust the angle with a small screw that is usually located just behind the top of the housing.

The mech must not move too far to either side, lest it push the chain between the freewheel and frame, or on the other side, catch in the wheel. Travel is limited by high and low stop screws, and the location of these varies from model to model. However, many are marked 'H' and 'L' and a little fiddling with a screwdriver will usually reveal what does what.

There should be adequate clearance from the big cog

High and low screws: close up   High and low screws: context

Run the chain to the small cog. If it does not get there, make sure there is slack in the cable (barrel adjuster). Then back off the 'H' screw, keeping an eye on the mech from behind, so you can see when it lines up with the outermost cog. Test. It may need a little tweaking.

OK, if you have two or more front chain rings, use the front shift control to shift the chain from the big ring to the next size down. Then run the chain at the back to the largest cog, using the 'L' screw to set the stop limit so that the chain willingly climbs up onto the large cog, but does not go over the other side.

Now, use the barrel adjuster to fine-tune the indexed shifting, so that shifts are accurate up and down the range. With a new unit and chain, shifts will go click-click-click, and with a tired unit and chain, do the best you can.

Derailleur, Front

The derailleur must be mounted so that the cage is parallel with the chain rings, and clears the large ring by 1 to 3 mm. Adjust via the mounting bolt.

A front mech also has 'H' and 'L' limit screws, usually on top of the housing. Run chain to large cog rear, and then to small ring front. If it does not go, check that cable is slack; use barrel adjuster if necessary. Then use 'L' screw to set limit so that chain readily drops onto small ring. Check that the shift is still accurate when the chain is on a middle cog at the rear — sometimes, when the chain has more slack, it will miss the small ring.

Next, run the chain to the small cog at the rear, and go through the same process at the front, this time using the 'H' screw and the big ring. Sometimes a front mech will have trouble climbing up onto the big ring, and if the H screw is moved far enough so that the shift happens, the chain may go over the top and foul in the cranks. Try raising or lowering the mech just a little. You can also give it a fractional twist, or off-set, so that the inside lip of the cage pushes a little harder on the chain.

Well, all is well; use the barrel adjuster to synchronise the shift control lever and the mech. You're done for this day!

Wheels

Remove/Mount

Wheel axles fit into drop-outs, and are held in place by axle nuts turned with a spanner or hex key, or by a quick-release (QR) clamp with a lever which can be moved by hand. Old-style drop-outs are smooth; modern drop-outs have a raised lip. If a bolt or QR loosens unbeknownst to the rider, the wheel will (hopefully) stay attached to the bike, at least long enough for the rider to realise something is wrong.

Before removing or mounting a wheel, disconnect the brake (see Brakes, Adjusting p.249 for instructions). If the wheel has a hub gear, disconnect it. If the wheel has a multi-cog freewheel, run the chain to the small sprocket.

1. Run chain to small sprocket

2. Open quick-release lever (pull away from bike), hold little knurled knob on other end of skewer, and unwind lever 1-2 turns

3. Grasp derailleur and pull back, so chain is clear of freewheel

4. Remove wheel

Removing a derailleur rear wheel

Mounting a derailleur rear wheel

Hold back derailleur and insert wheel so chain is on small sprocket

Guide axle into dropouts

Wind lever down nearly snug. Make sure it is in open position

Ensure axle is fully home in dropouts and wheel is centred between chain stays; close lever.

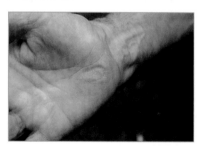

Close against enough resistance to dent your palm briefly

Removing or mounting a bolted wheel is straightforward; turn the nuts out until there is enough room to lift out the wheel, or turn them in snug and tighten with a spanner or hex key. When removing a rear wheel from a derailleur gear bike, hold the arm of the derailleur to the rear and wiggle the wheel clear of the chain. When mounting the wheel, again hold the derailleur arm to the rear and deftly fit the chain over the small cog just before inserting the axle into the drop-outs. Ensure that each axle end is seated fully home in the drop-out, clear of the safety lip, and that the wheel is centred between stays (rear) or fork blades (front). Wheel nuts should be tightened firmly, but not magnum force.

A QR mechanism needs a bit more technique. To release the cam, open the lever. The other end of the axle/spindle has a knurled knob. Hold this stationary, and unwind (counter-clockwise) the lever several turns, until the wheel can be removed.

Installation is the reverse. Insert wheel into drop-outs, then hold knob while winding lever clockwise. Make sure it is in the open position! When snug, back off a little and close the lever. The amount of force necessary to close should be neither miniscule nor titanic. There should be enough resistance to leave a momentary dent in the palm of your hand. The convention is to have the levers on the port side of the bike (left side when seated), pointing to the rear.

Rim Care

If your bike has rim brakes, I recommend cleaning the rims with steel wool or fine sandpaper. This is effective at removing streaking from brake pads, and other accumulated gunk. How often depends on how dirty; I do mine, oh, every couple of months or so.

Now and again spin the wheels and check the rims for truth by observing their position relative to a brake pad, or object held on the stay or fork.

Side-to-side and up-and-down movement should be within 3 mm; if greater, have the wheel trued by a bike shop.

Spokes

Spokes should be evenly tight. Note that rear wheels with multi-cog freewheels are dished to make room for the freewheel; hence, spokes on one side are tighter than on the other. If a spoke is loose enough to be easily moved to and fro, tighten it up at least snug. (Spoke key; turn nipple counter-clockwise.) If things have come to this pass, best have the wheel checked and, if economic, trued by a professional. Note that truing a banged-up old wheel is usually more difficult than building a new one from scratch. Nowadays, reasonably well-built new wheels are relatively inexpensive (about £25, last time I looked), and may be better value for money if the old wheel is tired.

Minor side-to-side wobbles can be corrected by loosening one or two spokes on the high side of the wobble, and tightening one or two spokes on the other side.

To move rim toward viewer

Use a spoke key, loosen by turning clockwise, tighten by turning counter-clockwise, and go a quarter-turn a time. Watch bobble (up and down)! This is much harder to correct. Wheel truing is an art, and it will help to practise with a discarded wheel before working on one you want to use. On the other hand, wheel building and truing is a can do, it just requires a methodical approach and plenty of patience. Game? Start with a visit to Sheldon Brown: http://sheldonbrown.com/wheelbuild.html.

Wheel Hubs

The hub shell spins around the axle by riding on round ball or roller bearings. One type is a press-fit, or cartridge, and is best serviced by a shop. Another type is the classic cup and cone, which is easy enough to service. If the wheel is on the bike, grasp the top of the wheel and push it from side to side. If there is distinctly audible/tactile clicking, the bearing is too loose. Spin the wheel. If it moves jerkily or roughly, the bearing is too tight, dirty, or damaged. Try adjustment.

You need a cone spanner. Remove wheel. Use cone spanner and regular spanner to undo lock nut from cone on one side. Hold the axle still with a spanner on the other side, and turn the cone in or out as required. Secure with lock nut and test. You want a very slightly loose setting, because when you mount the wheel on the bike, tightening the wheel nuts or QR will tighten the bearing.

Bearings run in grease, and hubs on an old bike or one that has gone for lots of swims may need re-greasing. The job is not too difficult, but guard against inadvertent liberation of ball bearings — once on the loose, they can be hard to corral. Proceed as above to undo lock nut from cone. With hand or lots of tape, hold cone on other side firmly to cup. Keep the side you are working on face-up, and remove the cone from the axle. Pry off

1. Unwind skewer and remove

2. Note orientation of spring

3. Fit cone spanner (has to be thin)

4. Use 2nd spanner to undo locknut

5. Hold axle in place (just in case bearings are loose)

6. Undo cone

7. Lift dust cover

8. Press fit bearing – for replacement, see a shop

Adjusting a Quick-Release Hub With Press Fit Bearing

Assembly is the reverse of the above. Set locknut and cone slightly loose, as the QR lever will tighten the adjustment — check when wheel is mounted on bike.

Adjusting a Quick Release Hub With Cup and Cone Bearing

1. Locknut and cone

2. Undo cone

3. Remove cone, be sure to hold axle in place from other side

4. Behold: cup, old grease, bearings

5. Ze filthy cone

6. Lift, fish out bearings with screwdriver or whatever

7. Hold axle in place, flip wheel

8. Extract axle

9-10. Pick out bearings

11. Clean everything

12. Grease cups

13. Pack bearings into cup one side, grease will hold

14. Insert axle

15. Pack bearings into cup

16. Install cone

From previous page:

17. Secure cone with locknut. Remember: set locknut and cone slightly loose, as the QR lever will tighten the adjustment — check when wheel is mounted on bike.

dust cover. You should now see the ball bearings, and hopefully they will be in a clip or cage. If so, lift out the cage, carefully noting which way it is positioned. If no cage, fish out the loose ball bearings and put them in a jar or other safe place. Turn wheel over, extract axle, and repeat process.

Clean everything in solvent, and dry. Wash your hands, else you re-introduce dirt with the new grease. Pack the cups with grease, not too much, filling the grooves is plenty. If the ball bearings are loose, hold one side of the wheel face-up and press the bearings into the grease in the cup. Fit dust cover. Drop through the axle with cone fitted, hold in place, turn wheel over, pack bearings into other cup, fit dust cover, screw down cone and lock nut, and adjust for correct play. If the ball bearings are held in clips (usual these days), assembly is easier because you don't have to worry about balls going astray.

Bottom Bracket

These days, most bottom brackets use cartridge bearings, self-contained units that are replaced when worn. Should be done by a bike shop. There are also plenty of bottom brackets with cup and cone bearings, but servicing requires special tools so again, have done by a bike shop.

Mending A Puncture

Remove wheel, as explained above. If you are on the road and have bolt-on wheels but no tool, seek help from another road user. It is sometimes possible to mend a puncture without removing the wheel, but at best the job is between difficult and !@¡#¡ZX!!!

Remove valve cap and depress valve to exhaust any remaining air in tube. Remove valve stem lock ring. Now — this is the key to success — go all around the tyre, pushing the bead (edge of the casing) away from the rim. Knead it around. Handle it. Get it loose. You want both beads down in the valley of the rim.

Insert a tyre lever under the bead at a point on the wheel opposite the valve, and take care that the lever is between the inner tube and casing, else the tube be pinched. Lever the bead up and hook the lever to a spoke. Insert a second tyre lever about a hand span away from the first one, lever up the bead, and hook. Check that the rest of the casing bead is nesting in the rim well.

The crux: hold the wheel in one hand with the tyre levers pointing upward, grasp the lever which is furthest away, and with a wiggling motion, push it away from you along the side of the rim. If the lever balks, try inserting it at a slightly different place. Most times, the lever will slide along and the bead will climb over the rim. Work the tyre lever all the way around the tyre.

Push the valve stem up through the hole in the rim and bring it out on the same side as the open bead. This might take a little jiggling. Once the valve is free, you should be able to simply draw the tube out of the casing. Hold it in the same position it had when it was inside the casing. You'll see why in a moment.

Mending a puncture

1. Let air out of tube

2. Move bead away from rim, all around tyre, both sides

3. Remove locknut (if fitted) from valve stem

4. Insert tyre lever under bead — do not pinch tube...

5. ...and hook to a spoke

6. Insert 2nd lever, about a handspan and away from the 1st lever

7. Position wheel upright, perpendicular to your good self, tyre levers uppermost. Grasp wheel firmly with one hand, with other hand (nose is difficult) push 2nd lever away from you.

8. Success! Tyre releases. Sweep lever all the way around the rim, to lift bead free of rim

9. Lift/wiggle out valve.

10. Draw out tube

1. Abrade tube around puncture

2. Apply glue, set aside to dry (this is a good time to check tyre casing for source of puncture, any problems, etc)

3. Peel silver foil from patch, do not touch sticky side

4. Apply patch, press firmly into place

5. Break and peel plastic film, working from centre

6. Use chalk and sandpaper to dust glue area

7. Inflate tube to shape

8. Insert valve stem in rim hole and work around rim nesting tube in tyre

9. Avoid pinching the tube!

10. Push the valve up and then push the bead over rim, into valley

11. Be sure the base of the valve is not caught by the bead, like this. It needs to be well clear, as in previous picture

12. Bead is seated right. Let air out of tube

13. Do top half, working with thumbs, alternating holding and pushing, as hands move apart

14. Rotate wheel, do remaining half, as hands come together. Last bit may be hard, lubricate with powder or liquid, or use a tyre lever — don't pinch tube!

15. Check valve stem is straight, fit lockring

Pump some air into the tube. Find the puncture. You may be able to hear it. Another method is to slowly pass the tube by your mouth; lips and tongue are sensitive to slight air currents. Remember to keep track of which way the tube was positioned in the casing. If you cannot find the puncture, pump the tube up harder. If that does not work, find some water and a container, and immerse the tube in water; the puncture will emit bubbles. Put and keep your finger on the spot.

(Sometimes the valve is leaking. Test by placing a drop of spit on the end of the valve. A Presta, fiddle with the knurled bit, but there is not much hope of cure. A Schrader can be tightened, but only with a special tool. A Woods, take it apart, and try moving the rubber sleeve and/or re-seating the insert.)

If your repair kit has chalk or crayon, mark the puncture area. Mark around the puncture, outside the repair area, else the patch will not stick well. Dry the tube if it was wet. Use sandpaper (repair kit) or something rough to abrade the area around the puncture. Eyeball the size of patch you will use. Apply a small quantity of cement to the puncture and spread it around over an area slightly larger than the patch. Set the tube aside to dry for a few minutes.

Use this opportunity to inspect the tyre for what caused the puncture. This is why all the fuss about knowing how the tube was positioned in the tyre. If the puncture was on the top, through the tread of the tyre, it was probably caused by glass, a thorn, or a nail. Look for the culprit! A handy way to do this without cutting fingers is to push a piece of cloth inside the casing and slide it about. It will hang up on anything sharp.

If the puncture was on the side, it may have been as a result of a thorn or similar, but could also be a 'snakebite'. This happens when the wheel hits something hard such as a kerb with enough force enough to mash the tyre flat against the rim. A full snakebite will cause two punctures, one for each rim edge.

If the puncture is on the inside of the tube, where it nests into the rim — trouble. We'll come back to this, but now, it is time to apply the patch to the tube. Wipe hands clean as best you can, and peel away the silver foil from the patch. Do not touch the sticky bit. Apply the patch to the puncture, sticky side down, and press hard, several times. More. When you are sure it is on, double up and pinch the patch hard between your fingers! What you want is to split the cellophane cover on the top of the patch. Reason is, you don't want to peel this from the side, because the patch might lift, too. Peel from the centre. If you cannot peel the cellophane, leave it. Now use the sandpaper and chalk to make a little chalk dust over the patch area. This will neutralise any glue not covered by the patch and prevent the tube from sticking inside the tyre.

Hang on, there is still what to do about a puncture on the inside of the tube. There are two likely causes, improper installation, of which more anon, and a protruding spoke and/or misaligned rim tape. Go around the wheel, looking down inside the rim valley for spokes that protrude above the nipple head. Any that are, file flat. On road, you may not have a file. See if you can improvise a temporary cover with a bit of cardboard or tape. Then ensure that the rim tape is centred in the valley and covers all the spokes.

Right. Pump a little air into the tube, enough to half to three-quarters fill it. Insert the valve stem through the hole in the rim and working around the wheel, push the tube inside the tyre. Reason for having air in the tube is to prevent it from folding on itself or otherwise pinching. Get the tube comfortably nested inside the tyre all the way round.

Let most of the air out of the tube. Start at the valve, and — important — lift the valve up inside the tyre casing, while you push the bead over the rim edge and into the rim valley. If the valve is not held clear of the rim, the bead may catch on it. Be certain that it does not.

Using your thumbs, go around the tyre, working the bead over the rim with your thumbs. Alternate. Hold the tyre fast with one thumb while pushing with the other. Let your hands spread apart. (If you keep hands together, then as you push down one bit, another will lift off.) Keep checking that both beads are settling into the rim valley. When you reach a halfway around the wheel, rotate it 180° and switch hand positions, so that your thumbs lead the way as your hands come back together. If you have done all that I have described and asked, you should be able to push over the last bit of bead with your thumbs.

If the tyre is a tight fit — some are — then use a tyre lever to get the last bit over, and be very, very careful when inserting the lever not to pinch the tube. It is much better to get the last bit of casing over with your thumbs, even if you have to heave and grunt a bit. Sometimes a touch of chalk dust or spit on the rim will turn the trick.

Wizard. Check that the valve stem is straight, and clear of the bead. Hold wheel and pull on casing to rotate if necessary. Fine. Put on the valve lock ring, loosely, just enough so you can hook up the pump and put in a little air. Make sure that both beads come up out of the valley and nest against the sides of the rim. Sometimes this won't happen until more air is added. Finish pumping, tighten valve lock ring. Replace wheel on bike, and remember to re-connect the brake!

Pedals

Pedals mount and dismount with a thin pedal spanner (15 mm), or a hex key. Grease threads before installing. Note that the left (port) side pedal has a left-hand thread and tightens anti-clockwise. It is usually stamped 'L' on the end of the spindle. The right (starboard) side is stamped 'R'.

Step-in pedals (for cycling shoes fitted with cleats) are adjustable for release tension, usually via a small bolt or screw. Double-sided models need adjustment on each side. There will be an indicator of some sort, usually marked '+' and '-'. Start with a low setting, and tighten as you become accustomed to using the pedals. Most models have cartridge bearings that are not user-serviceable. Any problem, see a shop.

Platform pedals (for regular shoes) usually (but not always) have adjustable cup and cone bearings. Dismantling a pedal is a good job for first-time experience, because the work can be done while comfortably seated at a desk or table spread-out with newspaper to catch ball bearings and prevent grease stains.

Remove pedal. Unscrew or prise off dust cap. Hold spindle at threaded end and undo lock nut. You might need a socket or off-set spanner for this. Keeping the spindle pressed to the cage, undo lock nut and then the cone. Inside in the cup will be ball bearings, usually loose. Get them out and into a jar or other container and count them.

Draw out spindle from cage, the ball bearings will hopefully be retained by the grease in the cup, but a few may drop down through pedal or stick to spindle. Be prepared for escape attempts. Garner and count.

Clean all parts with solvent and dry. Line both cups with grease, just enough to fill the grooves is plenty. Press the ball bearings into the grease. Insert spindle, replace cone and lock nut and adjust. Replace dust cap.

Cranks

Modern cranks are held with a bolt that will need either a socket spanner or hex key to tighten or remove. To dismount the crank itself requires a special tool — bike shop. To check if the cranks are tight, set them equidistant from the ground and with your hands, press down hard on both at the same time. Rotate cranks 180° and repeat double-press. If there is a distinct click, one or both of the cranks is loose; tighten ASAP.

Bottom Bracket

Most use cartridge bearings that are used until they wear out, then replaced as a unit. Older bikes may have traditional cup and cone bearings. Either way, servicing requires special tools, so if anything needs doing (bearings are running rough, or the axle is loose) go to the bike shop.

Headset

The fork steering tube is connected to the frame head tube by headset bearings. To check for tightness, lift front wheel from ground and turn forks. If there is roughness, the bearings may be tight or damaged, but check that any resistance is not due to cables snagging or other interference. A not uncommon problem is brinelling; this is when the cups and races have been pitted or dented by impacts. The symptom is that the steering (headset) tends to lock in one position.

To check for looseness, stand alongside bike, grasp both handlebars, apply front brake, and push bike to and fro. Distinct clicking may be from a loose headset, but again, check for other causes, such as a loose brake mechanism or part.

 There are two types of headset: threaded and threadless. The threaded type is adjusted using large headset spanners (size varies, may be 32 or 36 mm). Undo top lock nut, adjust race, reset lock nut. Sounds simple but will take a few tries, because giving the lock nut and race that final 'ooomph' to

secure firmly will tighten the setting; you've got to trial-and-error learn the right setting to start with. Be sure to use proper headset tools; pipe-grip spanners may bend parts.

A threadless headset clamps to the steerer tube, via horizontal bolts. It is held in place by the stem, via a bolt that connects to a star nut inside the steerer tube. To adjust, loosen horizontal bolts, then tighten or loosen top bolt as required. Only standard hex keys are required. Be careful not to over-tighten the top bolt, as bearings can be damaged.

A threadless headset is easy to service, because it is sure to use bearings held in a clip or cage. Just be careful to note which way the cage is positioned. The exposed balls must face the cup. Remove all parts, keeping them in strict order, clean, grease, and assemble.

A threaded headset is also pretty straightforward, but may use loose ball bearings. If you simply undo the top lock nut and race, the fork may fall out of the head tube, along with a rain of ball bearings, each intent on playing hide-and-go-seek as cleverly as possible. Bind the fork in with elastic cord or tape, do the top bit first, then either flip the bike upside down, or work over a large bin or blanket, to catch all parts.

Stem

The stem holds the handlebars. The type used with a threaded headset is called quill, and is secured via an expanding bolt which jams against

Quill stem adjustment

the inside of the steerer tube. To adjust or remove the stem, undo the mounting bolt 2 or 3 turns. To free the bolt, tap it with a soft-faced hammer, or hold a block of wood on it and hit that with whatever is handy. At least once a year, withdraw the stem and grease it. This helps prevent corrosion and the stem becoming stuck in the steerer tube. A quill stem can be adjusted for height; mind that the safety mark on the side of the stem does not go above the headset. When you tighten the mounting bolt, keep it on the loose side, so that the handlebars can be turned relative to the forks without undo effort. This way, in a fall, the bars will give and turn without coming to harm.

Wedge clamp

There is not much latitude for height adjustment of a stem for a threadless headset, because the stem fits over (rather than into) the steerer tube, which is cut to size. A shop may be able to use washers to make limited adjustments. Again, use the top bolt to set the bearing tension, and the horizontal bolts to secure the stem.

Seat Post

The seat post is held by a binder bolt; loosen to raise or lower saddle, and keep within the maximum height safety mark on the post. Once a year, remove the post and grease it, to prevent corrosion and becoming stuck. If this happens, let a bike shop deal with it.

Saddle

The saddle is mounted, and adjusted for position, via bolt(s) that may be basic or advanced in engineering and design. Either way, figuring out how they work is a simple matter of playing with them. Undo, wiggle saddle, see what happens.

Saddles last longer if covered against rain. A light, elastic shower cap works fine, so will an ordinary plastic carrier bag.

Seat post saddle clamp

Above: Top bolt

Below: Clamp bolts

Field Repairs

The chain snaps. You're miles from home, on an obscure back street that is not the best place to be, and you're facing a long walk. Is a fix possible?

Sure thing. It will be helpful if you have a handy kit of useful bits and pieces for repairs, but a broken chain can be tied back together with a bit of string (jacket drawstring?) or rag. Such a mend won't stand hard pedalling or shifting, but with careful use might get you home. Other possibilities include joining the chain with a paper clip, or parts from a pen.

Field repairs are a state of mind. You have to be open to improvising, and to looking around for whatever can be adapted for your needs. Urban environments are usually rich in resources: skips, rubbish bins, even roadside litter, can yield all kinds of useful things.

Spatial thinking is helpful. What use is a stick for fixing a broken cable wire? Well, if the break is at a mid-point along the top or down tube, it may be possible to tie each end of the cable to the stick, and limp home. No stick? How about a soft drink can? It's been done many times. Soft drink cans are prime repair material, because they can be bent and hammered into various shapes.

Naturally, life will be easier if you prepare for possible problems. Here are some items that may be useful.

» Spare tube — First answer for a puncture. Mend the damaged tube later at home.

» Tyre levers — Real thing is best, but a stick, pen, jar top, or even a door key, may be helpful.

» Puncture repair kit — You can have more than one puncture.

» Pump.

» Tyre boot material — If a tyre casing splits or ruptures, something with which to line the inside of the tyre over the damaged area, so the tube is kept inside. A bit of card. Duct tape. Excellent is a piece of Federal Express envelope — thin, but woven and strong. In a pinch, paper money!

» Hex keys — Whichever are needed for your bike.

» Screwdriver(s) — Flat and cross-head.

» Small adjustable spanner and/or individual spanners as required (8, 9, 10 mm are usual). Spanner for wheel nuts, if required.

» Electrician's tape — Pliable, and handy for so many things.

» Duct tape — Beloved of gaffers and other improvisers. Very strong.

» Few nuts and bolts.

» Length of wire.

» Zip ties, assorted — These are extraordinarily useful, and strong enough to temporarily mount a component.

» Small knife or multi-tool.

» Clip-on chain link and/or chain tool.

» Thin latex gloves — Just the ticket if you need to mess with a greasy chain.

MULTI-TOOLS

All-in-one tools with multiple functions are often cleverly designed for compactness, but check that a particular tool works with your bike. Sometimes, a multi-tool will fit or reach some parts, but not others. Always try out repair kit tools at home.

Having a repair kit is obviously sensible, but where do you keep it? You can't leave loose bits on an urban bike, and it is a nuisance carting such stuff around when you are off the bike. I am afraid there is no fixed answer to this question, because it depends on the bike and the individual. For my working bike, I've two-tier approach. I've stashed a few useful items in hiding places on the bike. Tape holds a couple of zip ties on a frame tube. In my carry bag, I have a good pump, and a small bag with tyre levers and a puncture kit. This way, I'm set to deal quickly with the most likely problem, a puncture, and can cope with others.

For my sport and touring machines, I often use a small clip-on saddle bag. These will hold a repair kit plus spare tube with room to spare. When locking on the street, you unclip the saddle bag and toss it into whatever you are using to carry your other gear.

HOW TO MAKE A SPANNER

You can devise a spanner from a bit of string and a piece of wood or a pen. Tie the string to the stick or pen, a little way back from one end. Wind the string around the nut, in the direction you want to turn it. Brace the short end of the stick or pen against the nut, and use the long end to turn the nut. This technique is particularly effective on small, hard-to-grip nuts and knobs.

On The Road

Tyre/tube Problems

» Tube cut beyond patching — you might be able to tie knots in the tube on either side of the cut, then keep inflating as you go. Dodgy!

» Tube useless — see if you can stuff the tyre with leaves, grass, rags, or whatever might provide enough substance for a s-l-o-o-w ride home.

» Tyre cut/ruptured — line inside of casing with a patch larger than the damaged area. Avoid anything sharp (such as plastic) that might itself cut the tube. Even a torn piece of milk/juice carton may work. If you have duct tape, then it may be possible to wrap the damaged area from outside.

Broken Cable: brake

» Possible to join broken ends using whatever you can find to bridge the gap?

» If wire still runs to the brake unit, can the loose end be tied to the frame or elsewhere, so that the wire can be pulled to activate the brake? This is less than ideal, but better than nothing.

Broken cable: Gear Shift

You may be able to bodge something by way of re-joining the wire, but it will usually be easier to simplify the system.

» Hub gear. If wire still runs to hub, tie to frame with enough tension to hold a low, easily pedalled gear ratio. No wire, see if you can hold the shift selector out with a pin.

» Derailleur gear. At the front, just leave the chain on the small or middle ring and ride. At the back, turn in the high-gear cage stop so that the derailleur is over a larger cog.

Broken Chain

A chain can be re-joined with string, rag, wire, paper clips, etc. A loose pin can be held by wrapping with tape. Take at easy on the pedals, especially when the break is under direct strain.

If the chain cannot be mended, it is still possible to ride the bike as a hobby-horse, alternately scooting with the legs.

Something Loose

Headset — Snug it down with your hand. You'll have to keep doing this, but will make home.

Crank — Difficult, because tightening requires a specific socket spanner or hex key. The very ingenious may be able to improvise a tool, for example, carving a hex key from a piece of hardwood. Another method is to jam something round into the hole, then push in a flat blade screwdriver so that the blade engages one of the hex edges. This may give just enough leverage for tightening. If you cannot tighten a crank, then hobby-horse, as riding a loose crank will soon cause expensive damage.

Brake or shift control, saddle, carrier rack, etc. Absent a suitable bolt, see what you can do with tape, zip ties, or string.

On To Victory!

We live in cities. Urban populations in Europe, Latin America, and the USA range from 73 to 80 per cent of total population. Asia at 40 per cent and Africa at 38 per cent are much lower, but their cities are swelling rapidly due to migration from rural areas and population growth. Asia, especially, has big numbers. Today, just over half of all people on Earth live in cities. By 2050, two-thirds of all people will be urban.

Cities vary enormously in nature and character, demographics, and size, but share a common feature; transport is lifeblood. The more efficient and sustainable the transport system, the greater the vitality of the city.

In developing countries, affordability is a real issue when creating new transport systems for cities. The infrastructure must be cheap and easy to set in place, and the system must operate efficiently and be sustainable at low cost. Notable, then, that few new transport systems are car-based. Indeed, the use of private cars is often actively discouraged or prohibited.

Cars do not work for urban transport. They use too much space. In London, 50 per cent or more of the land area is devoted to motor vehicles, but cars account for only 15 per cent of all transport. That's it. They can't do any better. Add more vehicles and the result is gridlock. Reduce the number of cars and flow improves but capacity diminishes. Either way, transport is not served.

Advanced transport systems use a mix of cycling, rail, and buses. The buses are not as we know them, and can rival trains for carrying capacity. A model for the world is Bogotá, Colombia. As well as a sophisticated bus system, Bogotá has an extensive and comprehensive network of cycle paths. Annually, Bogotá has a day when the entire city is free of cars. As well, every Sunday and on holidays, the main streets are closed to cars from 7 am to 2 pm. Some 2 million walkers, skaters, and cyclists enjoy 120 km of car-free streets. Bogotá now intends to bar the use of private vehicles for a total of six hours during morning and evening commuting periods.

Bogotá

New transport systems in developing countries often have the advantage of a fresh start. Cities in developed countries are already committed to car-based transport. They host most of a  global fleet of some 700 million cars and 300 million commercial vehicles. Broadly, car-based cities are of two types: dense and car-congested, or sprawling and car-dependent. European cities, especially older ones antecedent to the days of walking and horses, tend to be car-congested. Car-dependent cities extending over large distances mostly developed post-1950, along with rapidly increasing car production and use. The biggest are in the USA.

Time to home in on the UK. Britain's average urban population density is 10,600 people per square mile, only a little less than Japan, and nearly 4 times greater than the USA. No prize, then, for guessing that British cities are primarily the car-congested type!

To improve transport in a car-choked city, the first order of business is to clear space. London is famous the world over for imposing a congestion charge on motor vehicles using central areas of the city. The charge is successful in that it has reduced the number of vehicles, and thereby freed up space for buses and cycles. Bravo for a good start, but congestion charging alone is not enough. The charge is hard on people with low-incomes, less so on people who are well-off. The idea is not to make car-transport viable for a minority, but to improve transport as a whole. We need alternatives.

The UK's Green Transport Plan provides tax incentives which enable employees to purchase cycles and accessories at nearly half-price, with payment spread over a year. Naturally, the plan is rapidly becoming very popular. Here are two similar ideas.

Subsidise Cycling

Pay people for riding bikes. Such a scheme would profit the general community in two ways: through savings in transport infrastructure and service costs, and greater commercial vitality.

Decreasing car use means less expenditure on road construction and maintenance, traffic management, and health care for crash victims. The government Audit Commission says that road crashes (3000 deaths and 260,000 injuries a year) annually cost the NHS £500 million, and the national economy £8 billion. Just a chunk of that would pay for an awful lot of bike trips.

Encouraging cycling reduces health care costs in other ways. Cyclists are fitter and need less medical attention. And each 'one less car' reduces air pollution and damage to public health.

CYCLING AND HEALTH COSTS

Country	Bikes per 1000 people	Per cent of urban travel by cycling	Per cent of obese adults	Spending on health as per cent of GDP
USA	385	1	30.6	14.6
Germany	588	12	12.9	10.9
Netherlands	1000	28	10.0	8.8

From World•Watch March/April 2006.

On the commercial side, cyclists as workers are more productive and punctual, and take fewer absences for sickness. Cycling workers are a straight financial plus for employers. More generally, as traffic flow improves, overall commercial vitality increases. Faster deliveries and less energy consumed in transport means more turnover at less cost.

Subsidising cycling is technologically straightforward. Bikes can be electronically coded, same as an Oyster card. There are already lots of readers around, and it would be easy to add more. The clear link between cycling and work productivity means that a cyclists' subsidy could initially be for riding to and from work and school. A logical course would be to build on the Green Transport Plan, and equip participating employers, firms, and institutions with readers.

With time, the plan could be extended to other types of journeys, for example shopping, perhaps even trips just for fun! I can see cartoonists having a field day with the possibilities for exploitation, but as the saying goes, keep your eye on the donut and not on the hole. Cycling benefits us all.

Make Public Transport Free!

Public transport in the UK is expensive, because it is run on a customer-pay, profit-making basis, instead of being paid for out of general taxes. Consigning transport to private enterprise is a non-starter. A city exists precisely as a dynamic for the benefit of those who use it. Transport is vital to the health of a city, and is a community asset. All benefit, all should pay.

Free public transport would eliminate the cost of extracting payment from passengers. I'm not making a joke. The collection process is costly in both money and time, and retards the efficiency of transport.

Free public transport would mean a rise in taxes. Time to bite the bullet. Taxes in the UK are low in comparison to countries that are more prosperous and have higher standards of living and care.

The present system uses financial disincentives to discourage things that are not good for us or the community. Hence, high taxes on alcohol, tobacco, and motor fuels, and fines for the use of motor vehicles. Government revenue then depends on continuing availability of things that are not good, and outright exploitation of motorists. Better to tax and spend the money on useful things — such as free transport and subsidising cyclists!

Set Aside Real Space For Cyclists

One thing I'm fed up with are inadequate provisions for cyclists. Central government blows on about giving funds to promote cycling, but little of this is in cities. One reason: making changes in cities is difficult. There are many interests at stake. In consequence, even a simple task such as designating cycle routes through a park can take years of campaigning.

When it comes to making proper provision for cyclists on streets and roads, the problems of sorting out something worthwhile are so difficult, traffic engineers basically just fudge it. Painted signs and lanes are not good enough! Most urban cycle paths are a lot more dangerous to ride on than nearby roads with mixed traffic.

At stake here are lives. I accept risk when cycling but not the needless loss of life guaranteed by poor traffic design and management. The justification for 20 MPH speed zones for motor vehicles in residential neighbourhoods is a blanket objection-stopper: it saves lives. The same thinking applies to providing proper provisions for cyclists.

Most UK cities are radially-based, with main roads running out from the centre. Secondary roads often run parallel, or nearly so, to main roads. Traffic planners sometimes utilise these for cycle routes. However, for this to work well, cars have to be entirely excluded. This could be done on a rush hour basis, say from 7 to 9 am and 5 to 7 pm.

There is so, so much more. We need far better cycle parking facilities, and integration of cycling with other forms of transport. Take heart! We'll get there. Cycling in Britain has come a long, long way.

The 1930s were a heyday for cycling in Britain. The per capita number of bikes was enormous. Roads swarmed with cyclists, and with growing numbers of motor cars. The combination was lethal. Riders were mown down by cars so frequently, ambulances did not wait for call-outs; they cruised the roads, tending the injured and collecting the dead. The car/bike crash fatality rate was the highest it has ever been. But attempts to reduce the carnage were eclipsed by World War II (1939-45). Britain itself was front-line. People faced worse than being hit by a car.

After the war, Britain took to motor cars. Roads were built apace, for cars alone. In an era aptly described by journalist Nigel Thomas as the Dark

Age of the Cortina, bikes were shunted aside and only the indigent cycled. Bike production fell to an all-time low.

Of course, a proliferation of cars led to ever-increasing traffic congestion, especially in cities. The renaissance in cycling began in the 1970s and has never looked back. Continuing growth has been furthered by new designs, new materials, and improved manufacturing technologies producing better bikes at lower prices. Today, global warming and public health are major incentives for the further development of cycling as a fundamental transport resource.

For per cent of all trips to work made by bike, Britain trails well behind leading countries such as the Netherlands, China, and Denmark, but ahead of car-bastions such as the USA. We've miles and miles yet to go, but are on a roll. The growth of cycling is itself precipitating faster growth and development. The bike is winning because it at once is driven by and serves a wonderful force — human power!